Fire Island Saga

How The Barrier Beach Got Its Name

Illustrations contain a vivid historical
description of Fire Island's past.
Some images are in public domain,
or in private collection of author.
Engravings by Fred Juengling.
Selected paintings by John Mansueto.
Layout and Art Director, Dusty Grant.

HAND COLORED ILLUSTRATIONS WITH NUMEROUS MAPS, DRAWINGS, LITHOGRAPHS AND IMAGES

Author: **Warren C. McDowell**

Bay Shore Ferry Dock early 1900s

Cover: hand-colored photo 1900, photographer unknown

1

First Edition

Olaf Christiansen, 1887

Fire Island has a long historical background and is the largest outer barrier island running parallel to the south shore of Long Island, Suffolk County, New York. The island is approximately 32 miles long, home to Robert Moses State Park on the west end, Smith Point Suffolk County Park on the east end and the Fire Island National Seashore featuring an 8-mile wilderness preserve in the middle. Accessible by ferry only, there are 17 car-free communities, most of which are strictly residential with a few having downtowns which offer shops and nightlife.

Library of Congress Control number: (LCCN) 2019909499
ISBN #978-0-578-52121-3
Published by Review Graphics. Printed in United States of America.

DEDICATION

Patricia K. McDowell

Introduction of Author
Warren C. McDowell

Photo by Ted Lap

"Search for the truth is the noblest occupation of man; its publication a duty."
Madam DeStael Germanu Pt. IV, Ch II

Fire Island historian Warren McDowell shares the folklore of Fire Island and how it got named, its truths, myths and legends. From the Vikings, Dutch and English and the accounts of modern-day counterparts, McDowell's writing sorts fact from myth, and in the process may be said to kill one legend but give birth to the truth. It is perhaps always a little sad to see a legend die, but the author's account seizes a chance opportunity to reveal facts and events of the barrier beach so many years back, taking hold of the mind and imagination of historians. This book now passes on to a new generation of scholars to study these events that took place so many years ago.

Among many of his endeavors, his long-lived venture was in the summer of 1977 when he started a newspaper, *The Fire Island Tide.* His dream grew to 140-page color news magazine with poetry, history, artwork, short stories and community news. He also held positions as associate publisher of the *Sag Harbor Express* and *Shelter Island Reporter* and publisher/editor of the *Review* newspapers. His historical contributions and photography can be seen today in numerous books written about Fire Island.

Warren has an educational/business background from Southwest University and Indiana University with bachelor's and master's degrees. He is a lifelong resident of Fire Island making his home in Skunk Hollow, Davis Park and wintering on the mainland in Blue Point, Long Island. He is one of the original founders of the Lighthouse Preservation Society in 1980, with forty years of volunteer service on the Advisory Board and Board of Directors.

A decorated member of the United States Army, Warren also served in the New York Army National Guard. He received three National Defense Medals with two Bronze Star devices for Vietnam, Iraqi Freedom, Desert Storm, the Medal of Valor and Soldiers Medal for heroism, along with serving at the World Trade Center "Ground Zero" for three months and awarded the New York Defense of Liberty Medal. Warren's Military performance totaled 30 years of honorable service.

"Fire Island," is a name taken for granted for hundreds of years. Numerous authors claim to be experts on the origin of the barrier beach name, but many assertions are inaccurate. Since the passage of time, the name "Fire Island" has taken on a diverse and undocumented collection of labels. So too, the birth of the island also remains a mystery, including the original and exact date at which time the barrier beach was created.

Steve Levy
Suffolk County Executive
2004 to 2011

CONTENTS

Fire Island Lighthouse looking north over the bay, 1898.

Chapter IV

Margaret and Jesse Thoubboraon taking a dip, in their Victorian bathing attire, 1914.

Chapter V

PREFACE

Ocean swimming 1909 Point 'O Woods

he word "history" carries two meanings in common parlance; it refers both to what happened in the past and to the representation of that past in the work of historians. This book is an introduction to Fire Island's name in the second sense. It is intended for anyone who is sufficiently interested in the subject of how Fire Island got its name. To wonder how my historical inquiry was conducted, I relied on factual records of maps, surveys and navigational aids of the past.

The shoreline has been known through the ages by many titles. Long ago it was referred to as Prinse Maurits Eysland (Dutch 1600s), South Beach, Great South Beach of Sand and Stones, East Beach, Raccoon Beach, Restless Isle, The Beach, Barrier Beach, Fire Island, and, since 1964, Fire Island National Seashore.

In publishing the somewhat rambling and unsystematic series of papers in which I have endeavored to touch briefly upon, a great many of the most important points in the study of Fire Island, I think it right to observe that, in order to avoid baffling the reader with intricate discussions, I have sometimes cut matter short in order to avoid confusing my readers of popular legends, folklore, and myths in the paths of inquiry on how Fire Island got its label. I do respond in negative response to certain legends and folklore that proved to be more myth than fact.

Most assuredly Major John Andre's spy map of 1781 was first to record the name "Fire Island." Andre's contribution to Fire Island (though he was a British spy), was his pen and pencil spy map during the Revolutionary War which was the first to incorporate naming Fire Island. It dispelled many past and present writers who inaccurately wrote that Fire Island did not receive its name until 1789 by utilizing a deed recorded in Brookhaven Town. Historians copied past inaccuracies and relied on oral history to identify naming the barrier beach.

It is more significant to turn from the half-imaginary cartographic maps for the chronicles of the seventeenth century explorers. There is a flamboyant touch and a wholesome honesty about these casual records, which are most praiseworthy and refreshing, such as a passing reference of geographical locations, climate, land or the flora on the barrier beach. Alien from which every European anticipated, only to marvel these records, throw a strong light upon the fading image one seeks to restore. It will then help to reproduce these days, with a few disconnected excerpts that I give about Fire Island.

I have attempted to review the works of previous historians and come to the conclusion that only two have researched their work; others have what I call the parrot affect, repeating mistakes that past historians have made by repeating inaccurate history and making it a matter of fact. The only two authors seem to have researched their work, are Madeleine C. Johnson in her book, "The History of Fire Island 1650 to 1980s" and Harry W. Havemeyer author of, "Fire Island Surf Hotel." Both books are a must-read for anyone who is a thoughtful student of Fire Island history.

I look upon my book as a supplement to both Johnson's and Havemeyer's. There may be some difference of opinion on how Fire Island got its name, however too minor to mention. Therefore, the myth tellers recounted merely wonderful stories that their own families or others had told them, and had no intention of wrapping up a physical truth. It follows that many past historians were not bound to avoid incorrect truths in their absurd narratives on how Fire Island got its name.

Chapter I
Legends That Never Existed

"Truth is more important than old tales"
W.C. McDowell *Fire Island Tide 1977*

When History Repeats an Error

Fire Island Life Saving Service surfman surveying the barrier beach, 1880.

There is no primary documentation to substantiate the claims that there were ever five islands in the Great South Bay. The first time this idiom had come to light was in 1843, by Benjamin F. Thompson, in his book, "The History of Long Island; From Its Discovery and Settlement, to the Present Time."

Quoting from the same book, "David Willits, An Aged Man, declared that Fire Island Inlet was formerly called the Great Gut or Nicoll's Gut, sometimes Nine Mile Gut, because when it first broke through, it was nine miles wide." According to Thompson this event happened in the winter of 1690 to 1691, during a violent storm and at the same time a great number of whale boats, kept upon the South Beach were destroyed. Thompson claimed, "As late as 1773 the Fire Islands were called the Five Islands."

Now here, Thompson leaves us hanging and offers no confirmation such as a map, survey, deed, or navigational charts. In fact, if it is not documented, it is just an oral story! Thompson had not even given a written history of a name or names of any individual that made this statement.

Quoting Benjamin F. Thompson writing about his own first edition of his book, "The former edition which from the nature of the undertaking unavoidably imperfect." In his own admission there were errors in his book which included phases that were incorrect.

It should be noted that Paul Bailey, of the *Long Island Forum*, was critical and in his evaluation of Thompson's writing stated the following: "Thompson depended too much upon some of the hazy and old oral and undependable traditions that been told to him."

Richard M. Bayless book published in 1874, "Historical and Descriptive Sketches of Suffolk County," continues the echoing of miss information of Thompson. Bayless quoted, "Five Islands lying just within the beach opposite of this town, the original name of which has been corrupted to Fire Island, were patented to William Nicoll's June 4th, 1688."

Nowhere was a geographical location called Five Islands ever mentioned in the Nicoll patent or in the case of Nicoll versus Huntington 1805. Richard Bayless like other historians repeated an error made by Benjamin F. Thompson and in this case, he enlarged an incorrect statement by adding that the name had been corrupted to Fire Island.

NICOLL PATENT

On June 4, 1688, another patent was made to Mr. Nicoll which read, "For all those islands and small isles of sandy land, and marsh or meadow grounds, situate, lying, and being on the south side of Long Island, between the inlet or gut, and lands of said William Nicoll, at a certain river called Connetquot, in the bay or sound, that is between the firm land of Long Island, and the beach, together with, etc."

Whether this patent should be restricted to include the islands called "Fire Islands" only or "Captree," "Oak," and "Grass Island," caused an expensive litigation in 1805, between the trustees of the Nicoll estate, and those of the town of Huntington. Nowhere in this patent was Five Islands ever mentioned nor was it litigated as such because they never existed.

Historical Mistakes Made

Throughout our history there were numerous mistakes made by historians in relationship to identifying the name "Fire Island" and the fact that it was never used before the deed of Henry Smith of Boston, September 15, 1789. This deed was recorded in the town of Brookhaven on September 16, 1789. Once the spy map of Major John Andre, 1781, was found (which is preserved in the William L. Clements Library at the University of Michigan's archives), it generated the falsehoods of the barrier beach to be rewritten. The term "Fire Island" was certainly used prior to the Revolutionary War and was used during the Revolutionary War from 1775 through 1783.

In the book, "Suffolk County Tercentenary Commission History of Suffolk County 1683 to 1983, Town of Islip" it is stated, "Fire Island Inlet was not known under that name before the year 1781." This statement could be taken to task with the information we have today on the naming of the Fire Islands situated north of the barrier beach in the Great South Bay. Also mentioned, "Fire Island Inlet separates this beach from Fire Islands and the other Islip islands, largest is Captree Island. Since 1700 very little change has occurred in the Fire Islands. Fire Island Inlet, however, has been gradually working westward, and the Islip islands and the west beaches have undergone changes."

Here again is a conflict of dates; however the Tercentenary Commission now recognizes the name "Fire Island" since 1700 and makes claim that the inlet probably broke through the beach during the great storm of November 29, 1700. Other historians most notably, Richard Bayless, recognized that the inlet broke through during the storms of 1690 to 1691.

Shinnecock Lighthouse Mistaken for the Fire Island Lighthouse

A long-forgotten lighthouse on the barrier beach originally called Great West Bay Lighthouse existed between Montauk Point Lighthouse and the Fire Island Lighthouse and was activated on January 1, 1858.

Postcard mistake of 1905, the Fire Island Lighthouse sent all around the world. This blunder was printed by P. C. & Co. New York and reproduced in different publications.

It initially confused mariners who assumed it was the Fire Island Lighthouse.

This red brick tower at 168-feet tall was one of the highest lighthouses on the East Coast. During one stormy evening on September 30, 1883, an amazing one hundred and sixty birds perished after slamming into the glass panes of the lantern room.

The official lighthouse name was changed from Great West Bay Lighthouse to Shinnecock Bay Lighthouse in 1893. Locals referred to the lighthouse as the Ponquogue Light.

Shinnecock Lighthouse on the barrier beach 1893, sometimes confused by mariners as the Fire Island Lighthouse. Shinnecock lighthouse was demolished and removed in 1948.

Shortly after assuming control of the nation's lighthouses in 1939, the Coast Guard felt Shinnecock lighthouse was unstable and to avoid any more confusion with the Fire Island Lighthouse it should be torn down. In support for a skeleton tower to be built as a beacon, the US Coast Guard demolished the Shinnecock Lighthouse in the year of 1948. This eradication left only the Fire Island Light on the barrier beach.

Conjecture of VIER Island

Fire Island Inlet broke through during a storm in the winter of 1690-1691 creating the original four Fire Islands in the Great South Bay.

By 1659 the British had forced the Dutch from the easterly part of Long Island to a point as far west as Seaford and possibly Merrick. Through a treaty of peace in 1664, the Dutch seceded New Netherlands to England, but on July 28, 1672, taking advantage of a war between England and France, they repossessed New York and held it fourteen months and eighteen days before England recaptured it, thus ending Dutch domain in America.

Severe storms and high tides made many changes to the barrier beach. It has been established through testimony in the Nicole case of 1814, that Fire Island Inlet broke through during a storm in the winter of 1690 to 1691. At that time, it was called the New Gut or Great Gut and during the American Revolution it is said to have been a passage for privateers with attacks upon British shipping. Later there existed a Cedar Gut and a Gilgo Gut; neither one exists today.

In September 1973, the *Long Island Forum* published an article by Laverne A. Wittlock Sr., entitled "Conjecture on Origin of Fire Island." In the article he speculates that the word fire comes from the Dutch "vier." Since the Dutch word "vier" is pronounced with an 'F' as in "fear," it became first "fier" until attempts, for those not familiar with the local Dutch names, to pronounce the word resulted in reading it as fire and so spelling it. The drawback with Wittlock's prognosis is that in colonial times fire was also phonetically spelled "fier" and in early dictionaries, "fire" can also be shown spelled as "fier," as so in early English Bibles.

The problem with Wittlock's theory is that he utilizes the word "conjecture" in his story, specifically the noun form, meaning: "an opinion or conclusion formed on the basis of incomplete information." The verb form, means "from an opinion or supposition about something on the basis of incomplete information."

Wittlock and other theorists who tried to show Fire Island received its name from the Dutch vernacular are completely wrong. During the Dutch occupation everything east on Suffolk County was in control by English colonists. The important aspect is that the barrier beach did not break open until twenty six years after the Dutch left New Netherlands. It would have been impossible to name islands in the Bay that did not yet exist. It is a known fact that after the year 1650, the Dutch relied on English maps and it was not plausible that the English would use Dutch words in describing any new islands.

Fire Island Inlet and Five Islands

Trolling for Blues Fire Island Inlet, 1854. Note the lighthouse on the left, a stone's throw away from the inlet.

Most historians seem to agree the Fire Island Inlet broke through in the winter storms of 1690 to 1691, and this theory is derived from Benjamin F. Thompson's "History of Long Island" published in 1843. This event happened in the winter during a violent storm that broke into the Great South Bay. The Inlet has gone by many names in the past: The Great Gut, New Gut, Nicole's Gut, Nine Mile Gut, The Passage and Blue Point Inlet and since colonial times is now most commonly referred to as the Fire Island Inlet.

The "History of Suffolk County 1882" by W. W. Munsell & Co. stated, "It probably broke through the beach during the Great Storm of November 29, 1700 and was known as the Great Gut or Nine Mile Inlet." "Love and Luck," the story of summer loitering on the Great South Bay in 1886 by Robert Barnwell Roosevelt, places the opening of the inlet in the year of 1684.

It should be noted that historian Paul Bailey, founder and publisher of *The Long Island Forum* (and I may add one of the most respected historians of his day,) in his assessment of some of the earlier historians from Long Island, stated, "Thompson depended too much upon some of the hazy, old and unreliable traditions that had been told to him, because the script of his first three books of town records is very difficult to read.

A mistake once made is often repeated and so it is with those who were carelessly though unconsciously made by Wood, Thompson and Prime [naming some early Long Island historians]; they are still copied!"

Though Thompson made some mistakes and some were seemingly inexcusable, his five islands theory that was allegedly a mistaken copy taken from Dutch maps or charts that never existed. It is unknown where he got some of his material, but we know today it was inaccurate.

It is possible that Thompson may have had this misinformation of the five islands relayed to him by one of the local inhabitants of Islip Town. According to British Military Censes taken during the Revolutionary War, the total population of Islip Town was approximately 250 occupants. That said, many times local legends, folk lore and colloquialisms are passed on within families and communities.

British military with dispatchers sent to headquarters in New York City were very articulate in placing the Fire Island Inlet on record. For instance, on October 9, 1779, Captain Thomas King captured the British transport leaving Blue Point with 122 troops and seven Hessian officers within the Fire Island Inlet. On March 2, 1783, Captain Thomas Wickham captured the fifty-ton schooler *Peggy* leaving Blue Point for the Fire Island Inlet.

Another Fire Island Indian Legend

There are numerous Native American legends that are supposedly given to the name of Fire Island. Here we reprint one from the local newspapers in the Babylon area circa 1912.

South Side Signal (Babylon)
October 18, 1912

"In noting how Fire Island received its name the *Brooklyn Eagle* recently published the following romantic Indian legend, which has been handed down with other stories concerning both formal designation of this famous strip of beach opposite Babylon. According to old laws, the other Shinnecock Indians who inhabited certain portions of Long Island long before the days of the Dutch settlers in New Amsterdam, it was an offense, punishable by torture and fire, for any Shinnecock Indian maid to marry among the white people."

"Wa-ha-woa, the daughter of Big Frog, a wonderful beauty judged by Indian standards, defied all traditions of Indian law and broke all conventions of Indian folk lore by becoming the wife of a prosaic and squatty Dutchman, who had his farm between Canal and 14th streets. In the dead of night, at the last quarter of the Hunter Moon, a band of the Shinnecock Braves surrounded the settler's cottage and bore away the weeping Wa-ha-woa from the midst of her cabbages and turnips. It is said that they carried her away in their war canoes."

"The scarlet flowers that blossom and bloom with such exotic luxuriance on this island were supposed to have sprung from the tears of Wa-ha-woa, and ever since that time, by both settlers and Indians, has the spot been known as Fire Island. Whether this legend is true or not, the fact remains that, not only is Ocean Beach and all Fire Island overrun with the scarlet hollyhocks, wild roses and violets, but there is also a limitless profusion of shrubs, beach plums, blackberry, raspberry, strawberry and bayberry bushes, small pine and cedar trees and beach grass, all of which produce a beautiful variety of color, but with a preponderance of red bloom and green foliage."

An Indian tale of How the Famous Beach was Named After the Burning of a Maiden for Marrying a Dutch Trader

Wa-ha- woa Native American Maiden whose tears on the barrier beach created an abundance of red bloom and green foliage.

Seal Island: Often historians give credit for the term "Seal Island" to the Native Americans, because they hunted seals on the barrier beach. Benjamin Franklin Thompson in his book "History of Long Island" in 1839, alleges there was more than one island. However, the term Seal Island remains in the annals of the history of Fire Island.

Sictem Hackey: Quoting Madeleine C. Johnson from her book "Fire Island the 1650s - 1980s" "Native American name which appeared on the map entitled map of New Netherlands, according to the Charters is granted by the State's General on 11 October 1614 and 3 June 1621."

John Broadhead's "History of the State of New York" published in 1853, Vol. 1, which covers the seventeenth century Broadhead refers to Long Island as Sewan-Hacky.

The term closest to Sictem Hackey, in William Tooker's "The Indian Place Names on Long Island and Islands Adjacent with Their voice Probable Signification," is as land of the Secatogues.

The historian Martha Bockee Flint mentions an early name for Fire Island "Sierewhacky" which would be a variation."

Poison Ivy Did Not Contribute to the Name Fire Island

The notion that the Native Americans named the island for the burning rash they acquired from poison ivy, the shiny leaf vine grown profusely on the barrier beach is false. There is the same amount of poison ivy that can be found on Long Island. To suggest the Native Americans were susceptible to poison ivy while the Europeans, Dutch and English did not share the same fate is not called for, the myth seems racist.

Native Americans knew all about poison ivy, warriors coated their arrow tips with it, and medicine men rubbed the leaves on infections to break open the swollen skin and placed sap on warts to remove them. Upon first exposure, most folks develop antibodies against the sap, resulting in the bothersome rash. Other theorists made claims that the Native Americans, known as part of the Algonquin family living on Long Island had a natural immunity to poison ivy, successively using the ivy as a medical deterrent.

Native Americans handled poison ivy in many fashions as they were immune.

"The Journal of Immunology," volume 8 issue no. 4, page 287 to 289 states: "That the Native American is only slightly susceptible to poison ivy was indicated by the report in which states that though they frequently apply quite freely on their faces and other exposed parts, paints and dyes made from wild plants, berries etc., the skin of the indian is apparently almost immune to the poison ivy."

Since, therefore, the myth tellers recounted merely one of the stories, which their own families had told them, and had no intention of weaving allegories or wrapping up the physical truth in mystic emblems, it follows that they were not bound to avoid untruths or to preserve their narratives. In the great majority of complex myths, no such truth is to be found. A score of different mythical conceptions we get wrought into the same story, and the attempt to pull them apart and construct a single harmonious system, a conception out of the pieces, most often ends in absurdity.

One can still go to the Fire Island National Seashore or the Lighthouse and receive a lecture from interpreters that this myth is part of the truth on how Fire Island got its name, but nothing is further from the truth. In fact, there is more positive information on Algonquin tribes that contributed to the artful practice of wampum, whaling and dugout canoes that could traverse the bay and ocean, that would portray the Native Americans in a more positive light than some childhood fantasy.

Fire Island Viking Quest

*I*n the twentieth century there are voluminous suggestions that the Vikings may have explored North America as far south as New York and traversed up the Hudson River. There is also a date between 600 and 1100 A.D. according to the Norse sagas, they may well have sailed along the barrier beach. It is well documented that the long ships always attempted to keep sight of land throughout their expeditions.

In fact, the Vikings traveled as far south as Gowanus Bay in New York Harbor, as asserted by the British scholar Godfrey Gathorn-Hardy in 1921. The Vikings would have sailed past some of the paramount strands of beach, primeval hardwoods on the planet and unlimited fish and game.

This story allegedly was printed in the Minneapolis newspaper, upon researching this, there is a *Minneapolis Star Tribune* with no record of this story. Therefore, we place it in the folklore category and continue the subject matter for the interest of the reader.

"Evidence is mounting in favor of an alleged 13th century Norwegian Viking settlement in the investigation of the underworld discovery of what appears to be the remains of a Norse settlement buried off the southern coast of Fire Island. In October an oceanographic expedition led by the University of Minnesota found what was seen to be sections of a rampart surrounding a human dwelling."

"During a recent interview with Dr. Gustaffason who returned to his Minneapolis office on Friday, it was revealed that many other artifacts found, prove the settlement existed in the 13th century. Reluctant to disclose information regarding the investigation, the professor did state there is evidence of a dwelling with carbon remains that reveal a central hearth. Noticeably uncomfortable with the fear of revealing too much, the professor abruptly ended the interview refusing to comment in any way as to where the exact location of the site might be. Dr. Gustaffson did reveal, "The local authorities are being very difficult.""

The Fire Island National Seashore, when reached by phone, also refused to impart any information. In a statement made, they stated, "It is best for all concerned if the exact location of the presumed find is not disclosed at this time."

The last that was heard in any press release was the following: "Citing a new historical preservation site, the Department of Interior has declared as off-limits, a one-mile area of the Fire Island National Seashore."

Thus, ends the fact or fiction that took place in 1994 to 1995, leaving the reader to determine folklore or just another Fire Island legend. There is no doubt that the Vikings were the first to visually see a barrier beach as they traversed in their explorations along the coast of New York and some historians make claims that the Norse sailed as far south as the state of Virginia.

Skalholt Map, this document was written in 1570 by Siguard Stefansson a teacher from Skaholt Iceland. His original map has since been lost and thus this copy dates to the late 17th century. As an instructor in an educational center of Iceland Stefansson sought to depict travels of the early Norse explorers throughout the Atlantic Ocean. In a development that would have pleased Stefansson the map has helped determine the actual location of Norse sites in North America. Stefansson converted his information from the early sagas of the Viking explorers, as they did not map their explorations. Even then, in their sagas they recorded the new world 500 years before Christopher Columbus.

Sickette Wachley, 1655
Not an Island But a River

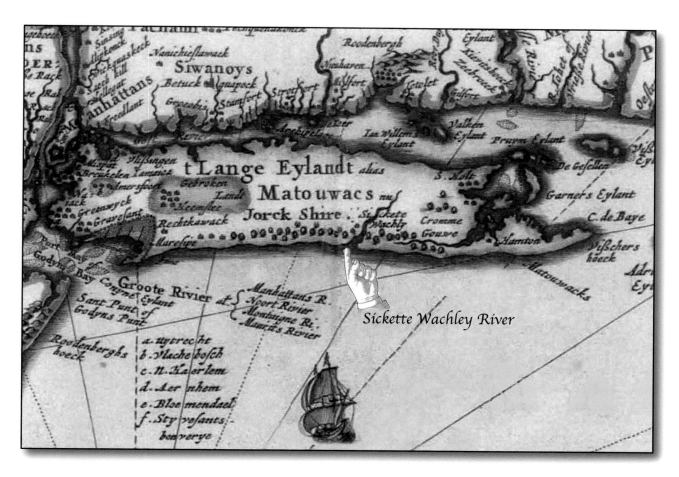

Sickette Wachley River

Detail of a map from 1630 with the "Fisher logo."
The signature is both the fisherman drawing
by N.J. Visscher.

N J Visscher map of 1655, though not showing the barrier beach, places Sickette Wachley as Carmans River, thus dispelling the rumor that this was an early name for Fire Island. Modern historians agree on the point that this geographic location on Long Island is a tributary flowing into the Great South Bay. Sickette Wachley, Suketewachly or Sictem Hackey appear on several Dutch documents and maps under various spellings. Take note that alongside Visscher's map, this river appears to be next to two dwellings. The symbols indicate both Native American and European settlements. Given the configuration of the river, it is almost certainly Carmans River, possibly north across our bay in the general area of Smith Point beach on the barrier island.

Scavengers on the Beach

Scavengers from the mainland of Long Island were notorious looters whenever a wreck was stranded on the barrier beach.

 History of Long Island; A Special Reference to Its Ecclestial Concerns, October 10, 1845
Rev. Nathaniel Prime:

Referring to the common practice of early islanders to appropriate anything cast ashore, wrote that, "There are men who would spoon the imputation of taking the most trifling article of their neighbors property, who would not hesitate, under the mistaken notice of right, to appropriate to their own use whatever they might find on the shore, without making the least effort to discover the rightful owner; not to speak up any direct efforts to conceal the fact, however derogatory it may be to the character of the good people, a regard to truth demands disclosure of the fact that a strange impression rest in many minds especially on the north side."

The Wreck of the *Elizabeth* in the Storm off Point O' Woods, July 19, 1850:

The *Elizabeth* was sailing from Italy, carrying a cargo that included marble, silks, oils, and soaps, with five passengers and a crew of fourteen. Many more curious onlookers and scavengers focused their efforts on combing the beach for valuable cargo washing up. Forty people from Long Island were later found guilty of stripping the wreck.

***Brooklyn Freeman Newspaper* Article, July 1850:**

Making Jest of the Arrestees: "It seems that the prisoners brought to New York by the U.S. Marshal from Fire Island, are so respectable that they refuse to give their names. The next step in delicacy will be newspaper notices something like this; some pirates were taking, who belong to fashionable families. A most worthy young gentleman killed his mother, we shall publish his name if he repeats the offense."

"Wreck of the *Elizabeth*, we blush for our race, almost to record the acts of plunder committed by the Pirates of Fire Island, on the wreck of the Brig *Elizabeth*. The lock of the trunk of *Margaret Orssoli* (commonly known as Margaret Fuller) was breached off in the trunk partially plundered of its contents. A desk of the late Capt. was found completely pillaged Mr. Aspinwall, we are glad to learn, was rescued one package of his imported pictures. Some of the manuscripts of Margaret Orssoli have been recovered and capable of restoration. *The Tribune* says: "Mr. Kellogg, the artist went down to Fire Island to attempt the recovery of Power's statue of Calhoun. He was furnished with letters from the underwriters, claiming for him every assistant that might be desired. Grappling hooks have been sent down and if the case containing the statues to be found there can be no doubt of its recovery. Mr. John J. Sproull, agent of the underwriters, has also left, it adds, to superintend the recovery of articles from the wreck."

18

Pirates Never Existed on Fire Island

It is not impossible at this distance of time to sift through the legends and find the true ones concerning pirates living on the barrier beach in times gone by. At any rate, setting aside all myths and folk lore, we have never forgotten the fact that stories about land pirates setting fires on the barrier beach cannot be corroborated in any documents by magistrates, sheriff's reports, courts or early newspaper articles.

In the year of 1982 the Fire Island National Seashore published a book by Ellice B. Gonzalez, "Storms Ships & Surfmen." And I quote, "The presence of land pirates is the most exciting but the least documented explanation for the high incidence of shipwrecks on Long Island's South Shore. When vessels became stranded on the beach, individuals as well as organized groups of people would rapidly strip a ship of its cargo and would often build fences and pig pens from the ship's timbers. To protect the ships and its owner's investment, Wreck Masters or Vendee Masters were appointed from 1787 to 1890 for each coastal area, most of these masters were appointed for the South Shore of Long Island."

This lonely pirate on the barrier beach was just a myth.

"Folk legend suggests that ships were deliberately lured to shore to obtain the wreck salvage by individuals called land or sand pirates. They allegedly lighted fires on the shore, disorientating ship Captains who believed the lights to be those of other ships and thus thought they were still safely at sea. The victim ship would come dangerously close to the barrier beach and subsequently be stranded on the outer bar, falling prey to these supposed land pirates."

None of these traditional stories can be proven. In fact, part of the legend of the barrier beach was that a man named Jeremiah Smith was a land pirate who lived as Fire Island's first year-round resident in the vicinity of Cherry Grove. Other stories have him living near Point O' Woods. The fact is that *The American Monthly Magazine*, dated August 1835 has one of the most visual accounts written about Jeremiah Smith, which places him near the vicinity of the Fire Island Lighthouse and that he was not a land pirate, (see 1826 "Fire Island Lighthouse" article page 50).

Two women whose names are unknown, allegedly lived east of Point O' Woods. They were thought to be a mother and daughter team but no documentation or written knowledge of them exists, only local legend. The mother and daugter allegedly set up a center of occupation to commit land piracy. According to folklore their dastardly deeds included murder.

The looters of the ship wrecks should have been called "scavengers" by the Wreck Masters or Vendee Masters instead of utilizing the term "pirates." The time for legends of pirates would be brief, with the coming of Lifesaving Stations, Revenue Service and the lighthouse on the barrier beach. With the invention of steam power in a world changing rapidly, the era of the alleged pirates on Fire Island ended abruptly with no documented evidence showing it ever existed.

Airmail First 1929 and
Second 1983 to Fire Island

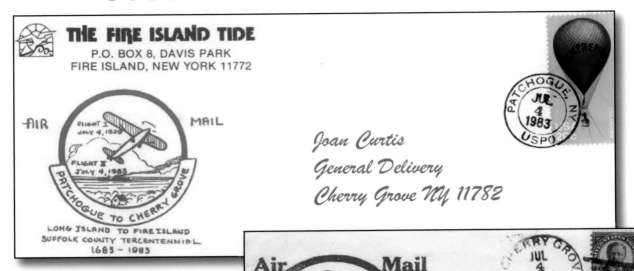

*O*ne of the corrections that must be addressed is the great airplane-speedboat race of 1929. There was also an airplane-speedboat race of 1983, many Fire Islanders tend to record only the great airmail race of 1929.

These are the following facts:

The airmail race of 1929, pitted velocity in the air with horsepower on the water, with the fastest claiming superiority as a means of transporting mail from the mainland to the beach. The first race took place on July 4, 1929, with Fremont Abrams at the helm of his Hacker powerboat, and Bill Hunt piloting the Patchogue Wings, Suffolk Flyers new Curtis engine biplane. The objective in the process of determining which was the speediest vehicle, was to deliver an official sack of U. S. mail from the post office at Patchogue to the one at Cherry Grove.

The airplane won the race just shy of fifty seconds and each carried a sack containing 1,750 pieces of specially stamped mail. In celebration of Suffolk County's 300-year birthday and fifty four years later, speed competitions still prove their attracting power. Hundreds of people gathered at the Patchogue Post Office, July 4, 1983. For the air rivalry, the 1983 match featured a 1940 Waco UPF – 7 bi-plane, piloted by John Schlie and co-pilot Ed Jansky.

Standing up for the speed over the water was Dick and Roberta Kavan from Kismet, Fire Island in their twenty eight foot mahogany craft, built by Sea Lyon of City Island in 1930. The Sea Lyon is very similar in configuration to the Hacker used in 1929.

The protagonists were escorted by Cherry Grove and Pines ferry owner Ken Stein in his 1937 Ford convertible. Ironically, it was Mr. Stein's father who, as a nine-year-old, carried the two mail bags to the Cherry Grove Post Office at the 1929 event.

The plane was cited first by the working committee in Cherry Grove, which included Jesse Morris, president of the Property Owners Association, and Jean Skinner the Grove's postmistress.

Even though the plane initially veered off towards the Pines, when it circled back to the Grove and made its perfect mail drop at 1:29 on the beach, it still beat the boat by three minutes. Signaling the plane to drop the mail sack were longtime residents Jack Sonshine and Nat Fowler; Dominic DeSantis president of the Cherry Grove Arts Project; Jesse Morris president of the Community Association; and Diana Stoller secretary to the Cherry Grove Fire Commissioner.

Both envelopes with the stamp of July 4 are collector's items and sought after, mainly because the post office is closed on July 4 and an error was made by both Patchogue and Cherry Grove, allowing USPS philatelic gatherers a historic day

Chapter II
Dutch

"The deepest truths are best read between the lines"
Amos Bronson Alcott *Conquered Days*

Brief History of Maps & Cartography

*C*artography is the art and science of making maps. The oldest known maps of the great south barrier beach (Fire Island). Most but not all of the oldest known maps can be found in your local library history section. Many libraries on Long Island have a history room and one has to dig through all antique books and old dusty file cabinets hidden away in the basements to find these early gems.

The Cantino Planisphere, which was the first world map, completed by an unknown Portuguese cartographer in 1502, is one of the most precious cartographic documents of all times. It depicts the world, as it became known to the Europeans after the great exploration voyages at the end of the fifteenth century and the beginning of the sixteenth century to the Americas, Africa and India. It is now kept in the Bibloteca Universitaria Etense, Modena, Italy. Unfortunately, it does not depict the barrier beach or any semblance of Long Island.

The old maps of Long Island and New York State were hand-colored by artists and provided much information about what was known in the graphic past. Maps are one means by which historians distribute their ideas and pass them on to future generations, from which they unfortunately at times glean distortions.

A map is a graphic representation or scale model of spatial concepts. It is a means for conveying geographic information. In the past, particularly in colonial times, maps were used as a universal medium for communication, easily in some cases, understood and appreciated by most historians and sometimes misinterpreted.

The sequence of maps depicting the Dutch Province of the 1500s, and the British colonial period between the middle of the eighteenth century and the beginning of the American Revolution is well-known. They were produced by famous cartographers, including: Lewis Evans, Samuel Holland, John Montressor, and Claude Joseph's Sauthier. High resolution images of most of the maps discussed in this book are available from the Library of Congress, the Stony Brook University, Long Island, New York and can also be found hidden away in your local library.

After 1650, the maps depicting Long Island and the barrier beach were made by British surveyors and map engravers. Dutch printing of all the maps of the New World after 1650 were copies made in the Netherlands of early English versions, whereas confusion reigned with the Long Island historians who gave credence to the Dutch maps of that period. Unfortunately, the cartographic maps were made in Holland, normally

The old maps of Long Island and New York State were hand colored by artists.

by illustrators who had never seen the Americas and at times placed and included was some miss-information from sailors who had once been there. Patriotic as they were the Dutch refused to print "New York" as it became to be known and instead referred to it as "Nieuw-Nederland" long after they had left the American continent. The Dutch seceded from New York on September 8, 1664 during the second Anglo-Dutch War. During the third Anglo-Dutch War of 1673 the Dutch returned for fourteen months and during the Treaty of West Minster which was signed in February 1674 the Dutch flag waved in Niew Ornje (New York) for the last time.

Map printing in colonial times was a comprehensive and complicated task. Printers brought their paper from a paper mill and made the ink in their shops. Paper was made from linen and cloth and the ink was made from tannin, iron sulfate, gum, and water. A single map could take up to twenty five hours of labor to produce. After the printing process the map was hung up to dry and all coloration was done by hand.

Adrian Block Map 1614

Dutch explorer, private trader, privateer and ship's captain

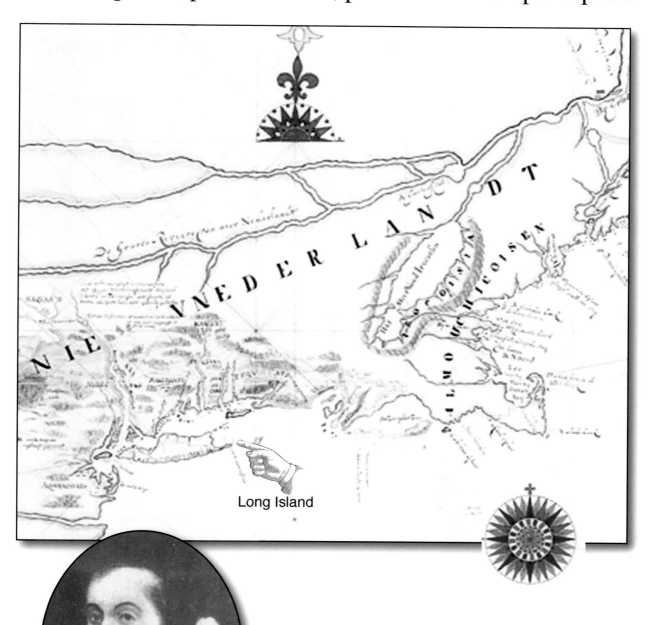

Long Island

Adrian Block
1567 to 1627

The first recognizable map of Long Island was made by Adrian Block who sailed around Long Island from 1613 to 1614. When Block sailed back to the Netherlands in 1614, a chart known as the "Block Chart" with his discoveries and questionable outlines of Long Island were recorded. Block, one of the few cartographers of the seventeenth century based his chart on observations made on site. Unfortunately, this map did not include an outline of the barrier beach.

Brief Description of New Netherlands

Author Adrian van der Donck 1655

During his career problems in New Amsterdam, lawyer Van der Donck experienced a fierce conflict with autocratic Govenor Peter Stuyvesant. He wrote a comprehensive report to the government in Holland in defense of his performance. That report, entitled "Vertoog van Nieuw Nederland" is one of the first books about New Netherlands that was written by an author who stayed in the area.

Van der Donck states in his book, "There are several navigable rivers and bays, which puts into the north side of Long Island, but upon the south side which joins to the sea, it is so fortified with bars of sands and shoals, that it is a sufficient defense against any enemy, yet the south side is not without brooks and rivers, which empty themselves into the sea, yea you shall scarce travel a mile, but you shall meet with one of them whose crystal streams run so swift, that they purge themselves of such stinking mud and filth, which the standing or low paced streams of most brooks and rivers of this colony leave lying, and are by the sons exhalation dissipated, the air corrupted, and many fevers and other distemper's occasioned, not incident to this colony: Neither do the brooks and rivers premised, give way to the frost in winter, or drought in summer, but keep their course throughout the year."

Barrier Beach

Van der Donck states, "Upon the south side of Long Island in the winter, why store of Wales and crampasses, which the inhabitants begin with small boats to make a trade catching to their no small benefit. Also, innumerable multitude of seals, which make an excellent oil; they lie all the winter upon some broken marshes and beaches, or bars of sand before mentioned, and might be easily got were there some skillful men would undertake it."

"Long Island, the West End of which lies southward of New York, runs eastward above 100 miles, and is in some places eight, in some twelve, in some fourteen miles broad; it is inhabited from one end to the other. On the west end is four or five Dutch towns, the rest being all English to the number of 12, besides villages and farmhouses. The island is most of it of a very good soil, and very natural for all sorts was of English grain; which they sowed and have very good increase of, besides all other fruits and herbs common in England, as also tobacco, hemp, flax, pumpkins, melons, etc."

Dutch man-of-war sailing into New Amsterdam.

Native Americans

Van der Donck records in his book, "To say something of the Indians, there is now but few upon the island, and those few know ways hurtful but rather serviceable to the English, and it is to be admired how strangely they increase by the hand of God, since the English first setling of these parts; for since my time, there were six towns, they are reduced to two small villages, and it had been generally observed, that where the English come to settle, a divine hand makes way for them, by removing or cutting off the Indians, either by wars won with the other, or by some raging mortal disease."

Sex

Van der Donck talks about sex: "The fruits natural to the island, all mulberries, posimons, grapes great and small, huckleberries, cranberries, plums of several sorts, raspberries and strawberries, of which last is such abundance in June, that the fields are dyed red: the country people perceiving instantly on themselves with bottles of wine, cream, and sugar, instead of a coat of male, everyone takes of female upon his horse behind him, and so rushing violently into the fields, never leave till they have disrobed them of their red colors and turn them into the old habit."

Prince Maurits Eyland Map 1682

based on surveys made before 1664, the seventeenth-century Dutch nautical chart of the coast of New York and Long Island were still identified as "New Netherlands." Johannes Van Kuelen first issued the chart in Amsterdam in 1682. The chart contains a separate inset map of the barrier beach called Prince Maurits Ely (Printz Mouritz Eylant) or one of the fragments of the barrier beach. By the end of 1656, four ships, the *Prince Maurits*, the *Gelderse Blom*, the *Beer,* and the *Bever* set out for the New World. One hundred sixty colonists had been recruited to set sail on December 25, 1656 to "New Netherlands." After having sailed in company of three, the *Maurits* was obliged to make this trip alone. For the sake of greater safety, a southern course had been followed for about seven weeks. On March 8, 1657, at 11:00 p.m., the *Prince Maurits* struck the outer bar. When dawn came the colonists found themselves within reach of the shore in an extremely bad position between the shoals and the strand.

One of the earliest descriptions of the barrier beach came from the logs of the *Prince Maurits*: "Before him they saw a broken coastline, bare of any trees or vegeta-

Johannes Van Kuelen
1654 - 1715

tion, fully exposed to the blast and winds." A frail craft was maned and many of the passengers were lowered into her. Amid drifting ice and through dangerous breakers, they succeeded in reaching the shore, making return trips as often as was necessary. Arriving on the beach, not a single piece of driftwood was found to build a fire by which the drenched passengers could warm their bodies. Historians have debated whether Prince Mauritis was a location on the chart where the shipwreck took place or whether it was the earliest name for the barrier beach.

On March 12, some Native Americans visited the shipwrecked travelers; from them they learned the place was called Secoutagh, Sichtewach and Sighewagh, which were the earliest known names for the present Fire Island, according to the natives. A rescue ensued by the Dutch colonists, and all passengers were safely removed to New Amsterdam.

Prince Maurice (Maurits)

In 1656, *Prince Maurice*, a wooden sailing vessel sailed from Amsterdam on December 21. The ship left Txel (province of North Holland), arriving and stranded at Long Island, on March 8, 1657. It was wrecked off the outer bar which is now known as Fire Island, N.Y.

Forty seven of the men were soldiers, many accompanied by their kinfolks; ten were bureaucrats and thirty-five were handicraft men. Seventy three women and children completed the contingent. Governor of the colony New Netherlands, Jacob Aldrich, whose history records as the exact counterpart of his nemesis, Peter Stuyvesant of New Amsterdam later came to the rescue of the ship *Prince Maurice*.

Jacob Aldrich also sailed with the party and recorded his adventure. Before the end of the second week in April, Jacob Aldrich reports an incidental report of the wreck of ship *Prince Maurice*, besides writing an account of his experience during his stay in the country. Jacob's Aldrich reports: "We proceeded with them on the proposed voyage, and after some storm and other obstacles, reached the vicinity of the Manhattans. Through ignorance of skipper and pilot who were never on this coast, having near the shore in the evening, she immediately grounded, and so shoved, which continued afterwards harder and harder, that we were not for moment, sure of our lives, and seeing no means of escape, in the morning we unanimously resolved to save ourselves on a broken coast, which we some days after understood to be Long Island (barrier beach). After all efforts to get the *Prince Maurice* off were futile, with every breaker the ships bow sank deeper into the sand. The heavy waves washing over the vessel, continually imperiled lives of all on board. A dark stormy night was spent by the ships company in great anxiety. No one could foretell what the outcome would be."

Thanks to twelve Native Americans in dugout canoes who crossed the bay, word was gotten back to New Amsterdam, recovery was made of all shipwrecked passengers and crew from the beach. Names of only two of the rescuing vessels are known. Company's yacht *De Endracht*, probably carrying Peter Stuyvesant, last Governor of New Amsterdam, and Captain Dirck Classen, were first to arrive. A rescue followed, and all travelers were without harm removed to New Amsterdam. *Prince Maurice* ruined in the surf and sank leaving no trace of her wreckage.

Compiled from: *Documents Relative to the Colonial History of the State of New York*, E. B. O'-Callaghan, Albany Weed Parsons and Co. copyright 1858, *Holland Documents II*, p. 8 – 10, 179 – 181 *The New Netherland Register*, Vol 1., 1911.

On March 12, 1657 Native Americans from the mainland, in their wooden dugout canoes visited the shipwrecked travelers and came to the aid of the *Prince Maurits* stranded on the barrier beach.

Arendt Roggeveen 1675 Map

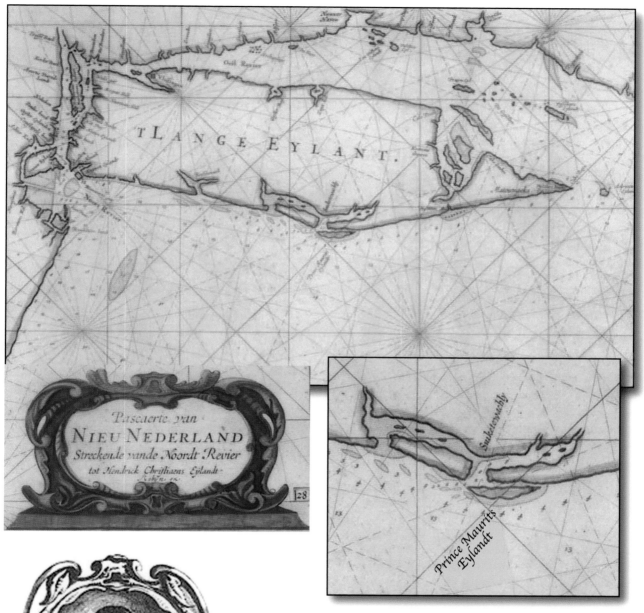

Arent Roggeveen
1659 to 1729

*J*n 1675 Arent Roggeveen produced a map of New Netherland which can be found in the Library of Congress. This chart appeared in the first publication of "Sea Atlas of the Americas." This was the first printed sea chart to focus on the shorelines of Connecticut, Long Island Sound, Long Island and the barrier beach. He was a land surveyor, mathematician, poet and teacher of navigation. Most importantly, Roggeveen's map shows the barrier beach in a different location than Van Kuelen's map on page 25. Included in both maps is Prince Maurits Island, giving more credence to the early name of the barrier beach.

Dutch Mercenaries Eradicate Natives

One effort to remove the natives and appropriate their land took place in 1644. The Dutch did not have enough troops to confiscate the valuable real estate on Long Island and the barrier beach, so they hired an Englishman called John Underhill to help them. Underhill was a very good mercenary and for 25,000 guilders given to him by Governor Willem Kieft, the largest killing of Native Americans on Long Island took place in an area on the south shore that used to be considered part of Amityville but is now called East Massapequa. He took the fight with his mercenary militia to the natives' stronghold known as Fort Neck and slaughtered 120 men, women and children, in the only major Indian battle on Long Island.

In the nineteenth century local historian Samuel Jones wrote: "After the battle of Ft. Neck, the weather being very cold and the wind northwest, Capt. Underhill and his men collected the bodies of the indians and threw them in a heap on the brow of a hill, and then sat down on the leeward side of the heap to eat their breakfast. When this part of the county came to be settled, a highway across the neck passed directly over the spot where, it was said, the heap lay, and the earth and that spot was remarkably different from the ground about it, being strongly tinged with a reddish cast, which the time worn people said was occasioned by the blood of the Indians."

European conquerors like John Underhill routinely use the Bible to justify extermination, and in many cases, the only escape from certain death was for the natives to reject their traditions and succumb to the European belief system. On Long Island and the barrier beach, Native American names were banned, speaking the Algonquian dialect became illegal, and performance of native rituals could be punished by death from hanging.

Many names alluded to Algonquin tribes for the barrier beach. One legend claims the Algonquin hunted seals and therefore referred to the beach as Seal Island, assuming they spoke perfect English, however *Brookhaven Town Record,* Vol. I Page 23, states, "Owenamchog was the name of a fishing station located somewhere on the Great South Beach in the town of Brookhaven, which differs somewhat in its component parts from the well-marked for Ongkouenameech-quke, the further fishing place. It is mentioned that in the memorandum on file as being the

Battle of Fort Neck where Dutch mercenaries eradicated 120 natives in the year of 1644.

eastern bounds of land sold by the Sachem Tobaccus to Setauket people in 1668."

William Wallace Tooker, 1901, author of, "Some Indian Fishing Stations Upon Long Island" quotes, "Enaughquamuck was an inlet connecting the Great South Bay with the ocean, now closed and its exact locality cannot be identified with certainty, as the beach bears many indications of earlier inlets. All the tribes or some say families belong to the great tribe known as the Delawares. Historians have listed various Native American monikers to describe the barrier beach and Long Island."

Before the Dutch colonization started, there were approximately 6,500 Native Americans living on Long Island, navigating the great South Bay and subduing whales on the barrier beach. An epidemic in 1658 of smallpox broke out and killed almost two thirds of the Native Americans. By 1741, there were only a few hundred Algonquins left. The settlers, who claim they purchased the land from the natives, forced them to move. After the American Revolution, Algonquins were rarely seen on Long Island.

Chapter III
English

"Sometimes we learn more from a man's errors than from his virtues"
Henry Wadsworth Longfellow

The English Takeover

Administering the Dutch colony proved to be a major challenge, and the English exerted more and more pressure because they were not content that this region had been claimed by the Dutch. England began to appreciate that the strategic location of Niew-Amsterdam was important for their further colonization of the North American continent.

In 1662 a new charter was granted in Connecticut, and this charter was interpreted to include the whole of Long Island. The eastern towns gladly availed themselves of this interpretation, and in 1663 the English towns under Dutch jurisdiction resolved to withdraw and place themselves under Connecticut (English authority). Soon afterward, two commissioners were appointed by Connecticut to organize the government in these towns; but it does not appear from history that they fulfilled their mission, and the unsatisfactory condition of things continued until the conquest by the British in 1664.

The populace, whose new civil organization hundreds of years ago formed the County of Suffolk were mainly English Puritans and a few of them Welsh. The boundary line between the English and the Dutch was established at Hartford by commissioners. They fixed the boundaries at the most easterly line of Oyster Bay, southerly and westerly from Huntington to the sea from 1642 to 1664. The English settlers were virtually their own masters of Suffolk County and the barrier beaches and owed allegiance to no one lower in authority than that of the British Crown itself.

Suffolk County and the barrier beach, belonging to the English Colonists, lends no credibility to any concept that Fire Island came from the Dutch word "Vier" meaning four or any other Dutch number. Historian Richard Bayles suggested wrongly that the name fire derives from a misinterpretation or corruption of the Dutch word "vijf" (for five) or "vier" (for four) islands near the Fire Island Inlet. The Fire Island Inlet was not even in existence until the storm of 1690 to 1691. The English, being very nationalistic toward the King's lin-

Not all the colonists were happy with the British takeover of Long Island and the Fire Island Inlet.

guistics would have not used any Dutch texts to describe the barrier beach in manuscript or other form.

The pressure from the English increased even more during the late 1650s, both politically and militarily. The English subjugated the Dutch with four frigates and 300 to 450 men on September 8, 1664, when the Dutch sovereignty in North America ended. The English renamed Niew-Amsterdam, "New York" after the Duke of York.

It has been well established that the inlet opened during the storm of 1690 to 1691. After 1700, with few exceptions, the most accurate and descriptive maps of the New World were produced by the British. A map published in 1700 by Robert Morden of London, depicted the island as it was to appear for the next half-century. The Dutch produced only copies of British maps from 1650 onward. Many later maps were clearly copied directly from Morden's without any changes. These maps prominently indicate the large, flat plain around Hempstead and the "sandbanks" on the South Shore showing the barrier beach as a peninsula.

John Seller Map
1666 and 1674

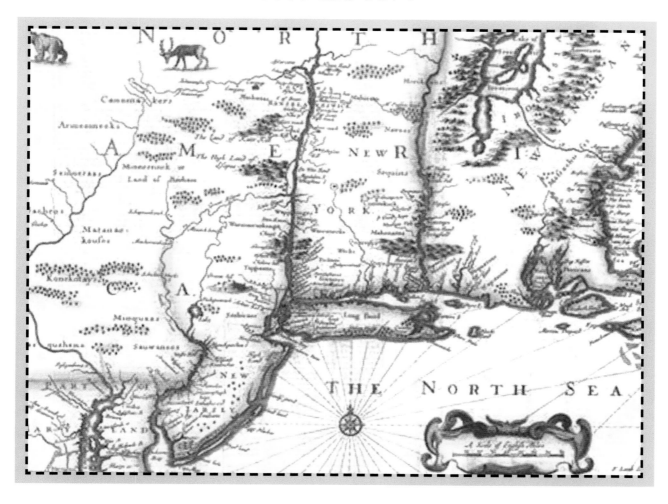

John Seller
1632–1697

*J*ohn Seller was a pioneering British publisher of nautical charts, he bore the impressive title of "Hydrographer to the King." Seller's map of Long Island was first published sometime between 1666 and 1674. This is the first British map of the New York area not entirely dependent on Dutch prototypes. It was derived from a variety of British and Dutch sources. Long Island south shore shows several features that do not appear on any previous printed maps including the outline of the barrier beach. Much of this information is derived from an unpublished map by John Scott. Scott shows only one inlet on the barrier beach, and that inlet must have closed sometime between 1657 and 1666. Scott's map portions are highly distorted. Unfortunately, the map was drawn from notes and memory when he went back to England, rather than the results of actual surveys.

South Sand Beach 1685

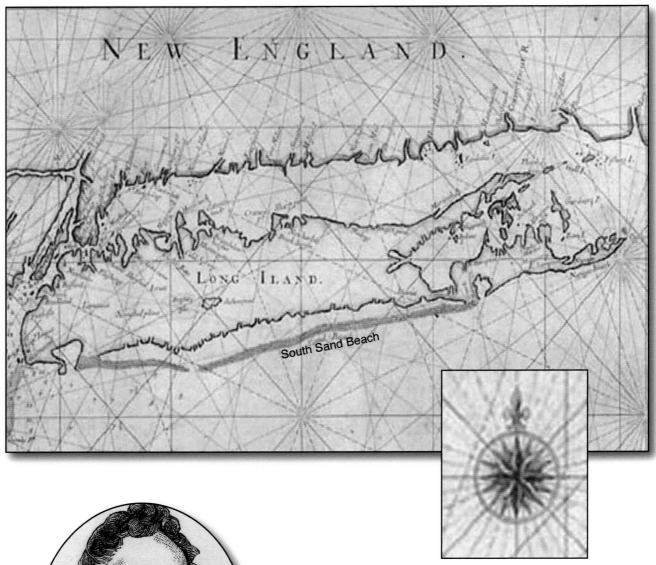

South Sand Beach

John Thornton
1641–1708

*J*ohn Thornton was a leading English chart maker, active between 1667 and 1708. Thorton emerges as a skilled practitioner both as a maker and possibly as an engraver. He was the first to make the transition from manuscript to printed charts, publishing three charts relating to the Americas or Atlantic in 1673.

Thornton went on to publish some of the most important maps of the English American colonies. He was the first map-maker to give a name to the barrier beach calling it, "South Sand Beach."

Forty manuscript charts and somewhat over 100 printed charts and maps by Thornton survive, earning him the accolade of the most competent and distinguished chart maker in England.

Maps Prior to and
During the Revolution

British and American negotiators consulted the 1755 map by John Mitchell.

The seat of action, between the British and American forces, or an authentic plan of the western part of Long Island, with the engagement of August 27, 1776 can be found in the Library of Congress in complete map detail. One of the most important historical time periods representing pre-twentyeth century holdings is the American Revolutionary War era, defined broadly as 1750 to 1800.

The eastern part of Long Island, specifically the County of Suffolk is lacking in the British military archives. After the battle of Long Island in 1776 the British Army controlled all the island and therefore seem to absence the necessity to provide graphic resources for researching the barrier beach and Long Island. However, we do know the British were quite aware of the Fire Island Inlet and utilized it to sail through to Blue Point, where they held a small military detachment. The Kings Navy also utilized a beacon on the Fire Islands north of the inlet to safely navigate vessels at night.

John Mitchell
1711 - 1768

Major John Andre, a British spy did make a pen and pencil map sketch in 1780 (see page 42), the first to show the Fire Islands. Given some of the impetus to create maps in the mid-1750s, it is not surprising that many maps were produced to locate and to assist claims to territorial possessions.

The topography on the revolutionary maps was second to none, and hand-coloring remained an important element. At the end of the American Revolution, British and American negotiators reviewed the map created in 1755 by John Mitchell to fix boundaries of the new nation and other nation's territories in North America. Mapping North America was a collaborative enterprise. To form a complete picture of the continent, European cartographers had to synthesize information from numerous sources, to form a complete picture of the continent maps. That test proved especially challenging because many cartographers worked in major European cities and never saw the territory they mapped. In the absence of their firsthand knowledge many cartographers drew from existing maps and sketches from other countries.

While these maps highlight America and Great Britian roles in the Revolution, they also document the crucial events that led from the French and Indian War to the War of Independence and on to the formation of a new nation during the last decade of the eighteenth centuries. In doing so, they provide basic graphic resources for researching North America's historical geography by mapping and reconstructing settlement and cultural landscapes that gave New York and parts of Long Island its identity and character.

Robert Ryder
"LIsland Sirvade" 1674 Map

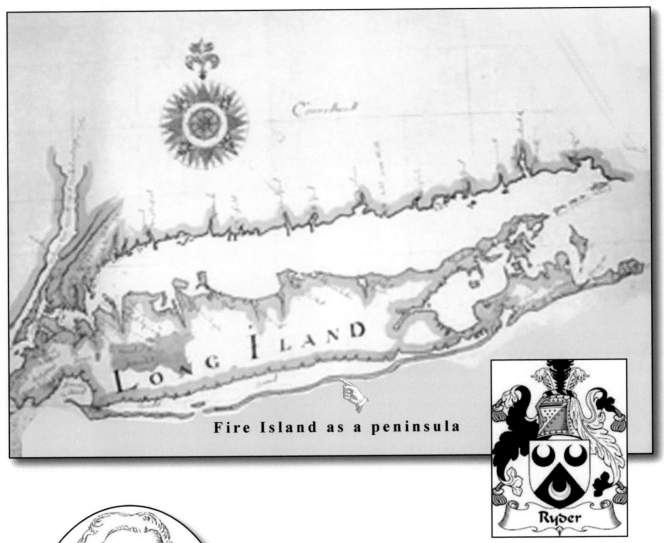

Fire Island as a peninsula

Robert Ryder

*I*n 1674 Robert Ryder's first map and survey of Long Island (LIsland Sirvade), was a major cartographic breakthrough. This was achieved by Ryder when he produced a private survey of the island as far east as what is now Riverhead. In surprisingly accurate detail, he charted harbors and bays on Long Island and identified the major settlements. Five years later, he drew an improved and complete map of Long Island and the barrier beach. Although it was not formally published, it was widely copied. Based on an actual survey, Ryder's rendition of the barrier beach is similar to the Scott map. His depiction of the beach seems to be fairly accurate, as he may have traversed it. Early maps were greatly simplified and tremendously distorted, with many of the island's important geographical features such as Fire Island totally omitted.

Chapter IV
American

Figureheads were a carved representation of the spirit of America on the bow of ships.

"History that is not documented is only an oral story"
Paul Bailey 1949 Long Island a *History of Nassau and Suffolk*

Barrier Beach Changing Shorelines

The changing shoreline could make it difficult to beach a vessel because of the wave action.

Fire Island's southern shore has changed greatly since the days when the Europeans made their first purchase of land from the Native Americans. The extent of the change can perhaps be better understood if some historical evidences are pointed out. Fire Island Inlet has moved more than six miles from its position in 1694. Some parts of the Great South Bay were once fresh water in areas, others were marshes, and still others, woodland.

Some surprising facts emerge from testimony in the Jackson - Woodhall Law Case in the 1830s. In that event, many old-time residents submitted affidavits to describe the bays and the barrier beach as they and their forefathers recalled. One witness, Jedediah Williamson of Islip testified that he knew a Native American woman in that place, one Hannah Jeltro, said to be approximately one hundred years old. Hannah said that people use to go across the bay by land through swamps. Other witnesses testified that when the ocean broke through the beach where Fire Island is now, it killed the timber standing on the Island which the bay now covers.

Jacob Hawkins, acquainted with the Patchogue - Smith's Point region, said, "That the beach in some places was 50 rods wide, there were swamps and good timber, and hills 40-feet high on the beach, he has seen signs of old stumps and logs on the water in the bay, standing upright fast to the bottom."

Hawkins continued that he had mowed around stumps higher than his head as he stood in salt meadows on the north side of the bay. He had heard that the bay was formally a swamp and freshwater and cited a Native American named "Old Eunice" who recalled drinking the water in the Great South Bay when she was a girl.

Other inlets once existed east of Pyro Inlet. Hawkins knew of two that had come and gone before the 1830s. Nathan Post described a channel called "Hallet's Inlet"as being from twenty four rods wide, open before 1795, enclosed before 1833. Nicoll Floyd, who had been Suffolk County Treasurer and the surrogate for thirty years, said that in 1773 there were seven inlets east of Fire Island Inlet; these were from a quarter to one half a mile wide and were located off Smith's Point, Moriches, Fire Place, and Mastic.

The Smith Point Inlet was some eighty rods wide, according to Nathan Post, and it was "a swift inlet, through which the ocean would roll into the bay and make it quite rough." He estimated the time of its closing as 1823. The dates would tend to support the tradition that the British used this inlet during the Revolutionary War.

From a situation of forest and freshwater area, to the other extreme of seven inlets, the barrier beach had changed still again in 1833. Then there were no inlets between "Quagg" and Fire Island Inlet. At Quagg the beach nearly joins the mainland. Richard W. Smith of Coram said that the beach was separated from the mainland only by a small run, crossed by a bridge. In the Smith family at Coram, tradition was that a man could travel from land to the barrier beach "horseback without getting his feet wet." Numerous historians and students claim in their writings that the barrier beach was originally a peninsula and until the first hurricane of 1931 created the beginning of the Moriches Inlet. The massive hurricane of 1938 separated the barrier beach creating an island as we know it today. Other inlets over the years have filled in and the Moriches Inlet has been dredged various times otherwise without the help of man nature would once again make the barrier beach a peninsula.

The changing shoreline is still very much in the news, and if history is any guide, there will always be controversy regarding the question of stabilizing the fragile barrier beach.

South Sand Beach 1708

1654 – 1732
A portrait of Herman Moll
by William Stukeley (1723)

*H*erman Moll was a Dutch cartographer who worked out of a London premise from around 1678, where he opened a book and map store. He engraved for a number of already established mapmakers, the most notable the chartist Captain Greenville Collins. In 1708 he produced a map showing the South Shore of Long Island, however the most important aspect of this map was the naming of the barrier beach as "South Sand Beach." It soon became clear that his work evolved into a distinctive style of map detail which was highly decorative.

South Beach of Sand & Stones 1755

Thomas Jefferys
1719 to 1771

nglish cartographer and engraver, Jefferys was one of the most prominent and prolific map compilers and engravers of his day. Around 1740 Jefferys went into business for himself and in 1746 was geographer to King George III. While not specifically a cartographer, Jefferys specialized in compiling and re-engraving the works of various cartographers into coherent cartographic wholes.

In 1755 he published a map of New England surveyed by John Green, and in 1768 he published a general topography of North America and the West Indies in association with Robert Sayer.

He is best known for his maps of America and in particular the American Atlas which is the most important eighteenth century Atlas for America. His work was consulted by American, English and French civilian administrators and military officers during the American Revolutionary War. In 1775, after his death, collections of his maps were published by Sayer as the American Atlas.

Whaleboats on the Bay

Whaleboats were used by General George Washington to patrol the Fire Island Inlet
and the South Shore of Long Island from Blue Point to Hogs Island.

The importance of the Fire Island Inlet and four islands north of the inlet, as beacons in colonial times was well known to the British military, and the colonial governors of New York. These beacons were aids in navigating merchant shipping and naval vessels into the Great South Bay.

Taking an article from "History of New York" 1879 by Edward Floyd de Lancy it reads, "Washington upon the arrival of Gen. Howe at Staten Island, in order to prevent the people upon Long Island from either, joining the Royal Army, supplying them with provisions, or conveying them intelligence. Washington sent a large detachment of his troops to the South Shore of the island and posted them along the shore from Yellow Hook to Gravesend; billeted a regiment of riflemen at Rockaway, and filled the bay on the south side of the island with armed whaleboats, small privateers and pettyaugers, that constantly kept patrolling the bay from Hog Island to Blue Point, north of the Fire Island Inlet."

After the battle of Long Island also known as the Battle of Brooklyn or Brooklyn Heights on August 27, 1776 the British won over Washington's colonial troops. The victory over the Americans gave the British control of strategically important New York City, Long Island and the Fire Island Inlet.

Contrary to belief, Quartering Act did not require the colonists to bivouac soldiers in their private homes. The act did require the colonists to provide and pay for feeding and sheltering any troops stationed in their colony. If enough barracks were not made available, then soldiers could be housed in inns, stables, outbuildings, uninhabited houses or private homes that sold wine or alcohol. This Act was a holdover from the Seven-Year (or French and Indian) War, and the

British reenacted the provisions of quartering soldiers during the Revolutionary War.

British military confiscated produce, firewood, cattle, and whatever else of value they could steal and ship through the Fire Island Inlet from Long Island to support their troops approximately fifty miles away in New York City. This did not stop the colonists from partaking in their own illegal activity, as there was no protection from Washington's troops, and the British seemed to look the other way. No fewer than 150 petty augers, schooners and small sloops were employed in banned business activities. They went miles sailing through the two inlets on the barrier beach Smith's (across from Carmans River) and Fire Island (located just yards west of what is now called Point O' Woods.)

According to British dispatches on rebel activity: "Fire Island and the South Shore of Long Island were still active: North London, May 22, 1778. Tuesday night eight whaleboats arrived here taken by Dayton, South side of Long Island." "June 12, 1878. Capt. E. Dayton, in an armed boat, carried three prized coasters into North Haven, which he took near Fire Island Inlet."

This bustling business went down the island and returned weekly to New York loaded with shellfish of every kind, wild fowl of all sorts, and in winter with large quantities of fish with which the New York markets were plentifully supplied. They also used to carry such merchandise as was suitable to country people, which they bartered away for hogs, lambs, calves and other merchandise.

Not until prohibition took place in the Roaring 20s did Fire Island and the inlet see such a bustle of illegal activity, some referred it to bootleggers.

The War of 1812

British continually sailed along the barrier beach during the Revolutionary War and the War of 1812.

During the War of 1812, the coast of the barrier beach and the south coast of Long Island were in a very unprotected condition. British man-of-war daily cruised from Sandy Hook to Montauk in sight of the shore, seizing small coasting vessels and occasionally landing on the mainland of Suffolk County and carrying away supplies. The inhabitants upon this as well as other parts of the coast were frequently distressed by the reports which prevailed of the landing of troops from the British ships.

Of all the causes for the War of 1812, the impressment of American sailors into the Royal Navy was the most important for many Americans, especially those who lived along the shore of Long Island. The British naval practice of manning ships with pressed men, who were forcibly placed into service, was a common one in English history, dating back to medieval times.

On one occasion the apprehension of the Royal Navy's impressment of citizens sailing along the South Shore and the barrier beach raised an alarm. Long Island's local militia was called out, but the alarm, like many others proved groundless. A new schooner, owned by Benjamin Rushmore and Simon W. Cooper, was called the *Fair Trader*. In command was Captain Richard Jackson and the vessel was loaded with a valuable cargo. This ship was captured near the inlet by an English party sent in a barge from one of Admiral George Cockburn's ships.

Sir George Cockburn (10th Baronet) also directed the capture and burning of Washington, D.C., on August 24, 1814 as an advisor to Major General Robert Ross during the War of 1812. He went on to be the First Naval Lord in the British Navy.

Desertions from sailors on British war vessels when cruising along the coast were not infrequent. Several of the deserters became residents of Long Island. One of them, Thomas H. Derverell became a school teacher in the village of Babylon. As flogging was part of discipline, for sailors from British man-of-war, desertions became more frequent, as they traversed the barrier beach and made their way to the mainland.

Barrier Beach Ship Trap

A slender ribbon of sand parallels the south shore of Long Island's ever-changing shoreline and shoals, making new inlets and closing others. The shoreline has been known through the ages by many titles. Although it has many applications at various locations, we know it in general today as Fire Island or simply "The Beach." Upon this barrier beach, hundreds of ships and untold numbers of passengers have become victims of a trap. The treachery caused the toll to become well-known in maritime circles and history. The United States Life-Saving Service was established in 1878 with their rescue stations in very close proximity, approximately 12 miles apart all along the length of the island.

Upon the barrier beach, hundreds of ships and untold numbers of victims became caught in what became known as the Fire Island ship trap.

One hundred twenty-five years ago, walking across the desolate strip of beach, a hiker would come across dunes as high as forty feet lining the ocean front. Climbing the height of the dunes you would see spread before you an astonishing sight. At the foot of the dunes, wreck after wreck lay quietly, as though mortally wounded after a hard struggle. They laid mainly bow into the dunes. Some were very old and bleached and weathered by many years of exposure. Others still showed signs of pain and not completely rusted bolts and fittings. Some displayed only ribs and a portion of keel, deeply embedded in sand, while the next might still boast another planking to indicate the shape of the hull.

In between the wrecks, timbers and broken spars lay separately or in amazingly neat piles as though the God Neptune wished to make amends for the havoc he had wrought. Of blocks or tackle, ropes or hawsers or light spars, there would be none. Beachcombers and scavengers from the mainland, or wreckers had been there to make claim of anything of value. If this visit were on a bright and windless day, the hiker would note a thin line of breakers well offshore and shimmering white against the dark blue background of the ocean. Between this line and the shore small vessels could be maneuvered in calm water with complete safety. Between this peaceful panorama and innocuous stretch of beach, Mother Nature had formed a perfect deadly *ship trap*.

Approximately a quarter of a mile off the beach lies a sandbar that stretches in an almost identical line with the beach itself. The depth of the water on the bar varies between six and nine feet, although at certain times it may be less than hip high. Naturally, heavy seas break on the bar and cascade over into a depth of about twenty feet then it gradually settles and shallows into the beach. Beyond the bar the debth of the ocean falls off rapidly into water several fathoms deep. Most of the ships wrecked on Fire Island have first struck the bar, often snapping their masts at the impact. Small vessels were often lifted over the bar when the sea was heavy enough. In the case of large vessels they would be torn to pieces as they lay exposed to the full might of the Atlantic Ocean.

During the winter and particularly subzero temperature conditions when most of the bad wrecks occurred, the trap worked to its perfection. Now snow-blinded vessels stranded on the sand bar had become unmanageable, flanked between the bar and the beach, unable to set the craft free.

By now wrecks have almost disappeared, but on certain days when the tide goes out, skeletons of these ruins can be seen. Still on a wild night when the ocean roars and the spray flies inland, one can sense the peril of the Fire Island of old.

Major John André Spy Map 1781

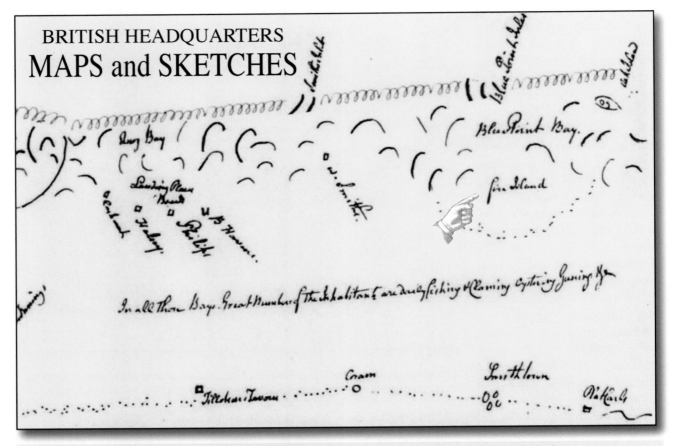

A pencil sketch of the outline of the south shore of Long Island, showing the bar in front of the Great South Bay and the inlets through the bar.

A pencil and ink sketch of the South Shore of Long Island is shown depicting the barrier beach in front of the Great South Bay and the inlets through the bar. There are notations of property holders along the shore and relative position of towns such as Smithtown.

Major John Andre was a spy used by British headquarters for Sir Henry Clinton, while in command of the British forces operating in North America, during the War for Independence 1755 to 1782. Unfortunately, due to the period, most of the outlines of the barrier beach and Long Island have faded to the point of being unrecognizable. However, the locations done in ink are very recognizable.

This map is the first to show the name Fire Island (now known as West Island), taking note that this island was in the bay and not the barrier beach. He also outlines the inlets as Smith's Inlet and the Blue Point Inlet. I believe Blue Point Inlet was more of the navigational finder. Later the British military identified Blue Point inlet as the Fire Island Inlet. Blue Point

was an important British port on the South Shore of Long Island, with British and Hessians troops bivouacking there to protect confiscated goods taken from the local inhabitants

Reports have been taken about rebels by a British officer during the American Revolution. An excellent source of information on the Revolutionary War can be found in, *Revolutionary Incidents of Suffolk and Kings Counties*; with an account of the Battle of Long Island.

British Dispatches:

May 25, 1778: "Four more whaleboats have again made their appearance in Blue Point Bay and intend to prevent any boats resorting thither; they lay on the beach and get necessities from the inhabitants in that neighborhood."

June 15, 1778: "Capt. E. Dayton, in an armed boat, carried three prizes (coasters) into N. Haven, which he took near Fire Island Inlet."

Capt. Dayton was a renowned American privateer who inflicted much damage to His Majesty's British Navy. It was quite evident during the American Revolution that the British had recognized the Fire Island Inlet as a passageway to the south shore of Long Island. Major Andre more than likely named Fire Island from the native Long Islanders, as this island was used to bring vessels through the inlet at night. The colonial governor prior to the revolution had commissioned Native Americans to light beacon's so ships and smaller vessels could make their way through the inlet. The British military had more sophisticated beacons that were used not only on Fire Island but also utilized at Montauk Point to ward off ships of the line from running aground at Montauk.

In 1779 Andre became the adjutant general of the British Army. This was one of the senior-most administrative positions overseeing personnel issues and policies. In this role, Andre was given charge of the British intelligence program and then became involved in the Benedict Arnold Affair.

General George Washington offered British General Clinton to exchange Andre for Benedict Arnold, hoping to hang Arnold for his treason. Clinton failed to respond and allowed Andre to hang from the gallows. After his death, Andre was buried at the foot of the gallows. In 1821, Andre's body was removed to

England and buried in Westminster Abbey as a hero.

Andre's contribution to the mapping of Fire Island, even though he was a British spy and his sketch is not known for complete accuracy, is one of the first maps to incorporate the name "Fire Island." This dispelled many of historian's inaccurate naming of the Fire Island.

The figure of the Beacon appears thus from the "Pictoral Field Book" of the Revolution by Benson John Lossing.

John Andre, 1750-1780.
British Army officer hanged as a spy during the American Revolutionary War.

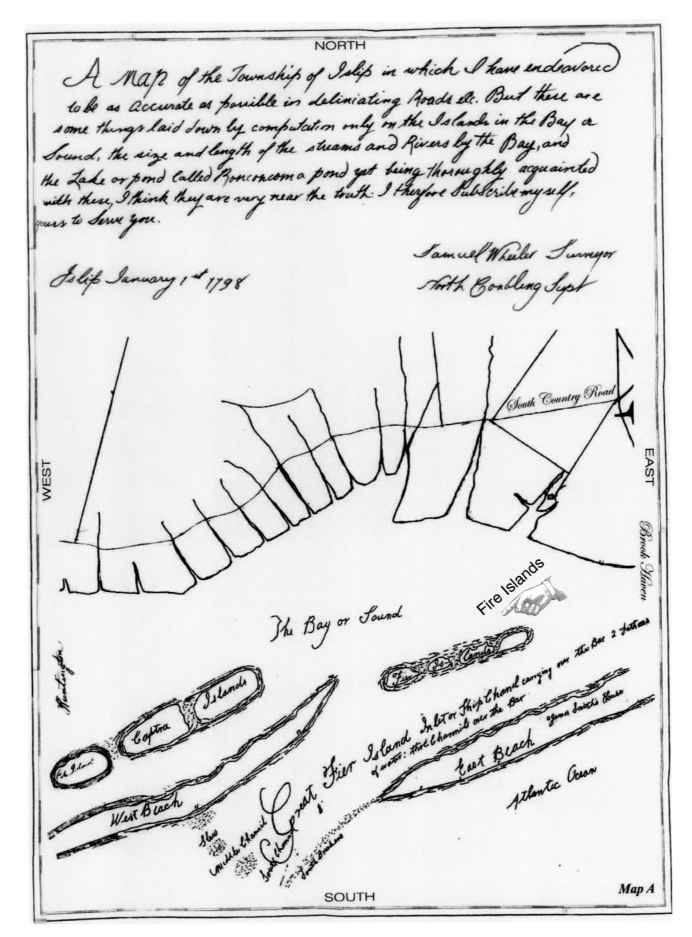

NORTH

A Map of the Township of Islip in which I have endeavored to be as Accurate as possible in deliniating Roads &c. But there are some things laid down by computation only viz the Islands in the Bay or Sound, the size and length of the streams and Rivers by the Bay, and the Lake or pond called Ronconcom a pond yet being thoroughly acquainted with these, I think they are very near the truth. I therfore Subscribe myself, yours to Serve you.

Islip January 1st 1798

Samuel Wheeler Surveyor
North Combling Syst

WEST

EAST

South Country Road

Brook Haven

The Bay or Sound

Fire Islands

Huntington

Islands

Captree

Fir Island

Fire Is Islands

West Beach

Sloo

Middle Channel

South Channel

Great Fier Island Inlet or Ship Chanl carrying over the Bar 2 fathoms of water: three & a half miles over the Bar

East Beach

John Smith's House

Atlantic Ocean

SOUTH

Map A

Samuel Wheeler 1798

*S*amuel Wheeler's map of Islip, 1798 is found in files of the surveyor general in a vault in the Department of Public Works of the State Assembly of New York at Albany. They are badly discolored by age and quite frayed from passage from hand to hand for many years. It was possible to obtain excellent photo stats of four heavy sheets that make up the whole map. A more intriguing and interesting document can be found, establishing the Fire Islands, East Island and inlets.

According to the best authorities it settles once and for all, the disputes about the original name of today's Fire Island. It was known as East Beach in the Wheeler's Map of 1798. Fire Island was derived from a chain of four islands which lay practically across the inlet.

It was obvious that the draftsman had added his fieldnotes and lettering on whichever side he happened to be on. One must take time to decipher the fine script. This was a most unusual method used in drawing and lettering the map of Islip Town.

Word phrases and long-forgotten terms cover the surface in describing the inlet which is referred to as Great Fier Island Inlet or Ship Channel. The lettering advises that it is carrying two fathoms of water over the bar and shows that in 1798, there were three passages through the inlet: a South Channel, Middle Channel, and a Slew. One particular piece of interest is the fact that this map shows a house on the island labeled, "James Smith house."

There's been much controversy over the spelling of Fire Island. Wheeler spells it phonetically "Fier" which was not uncommon for colonial times. In a brief description of New York formally called New Netherlands 1670, quoting an example of the spelling of fire, "Does shade and shelter them from the scorching beams of souls fiery influence." Lake Ronkonkoma is indicated phonetically as "Rocconcoma." The great South Bay is shown as the Bay or Sound.

Granting that Samuel Wheeler's map, survey

Surveying on the barrier beach was not an easy task in 1798.

Samuel Wheeler
1762 - 1845

establishes a fact that the name "Fire Island" belonged to the four islands, and not to the area now known by that title today. Much in evidence in the year about 1770 that then Royal Gov. of New York, tiring of the loss of ships and men along the outer beach made a contract with local native tribes. The contract included to light beacon fires on the islands to guide ships into safer waters of the bay. This leads to more credence that the name "Fire Island" derived from lighted beacons on the islands in the bay.

From 1800 to 1802 the Islip records show that Samuel Wheeler was appointed as Fence Viewer. The fence viewer in colonial times is a town or city official who administers fence laws by inspecting new fence and settlements of disputes arising from trespass by livestock that have escaped enclosures.

1797 Map of the Town of Brookhaven and Fire Island

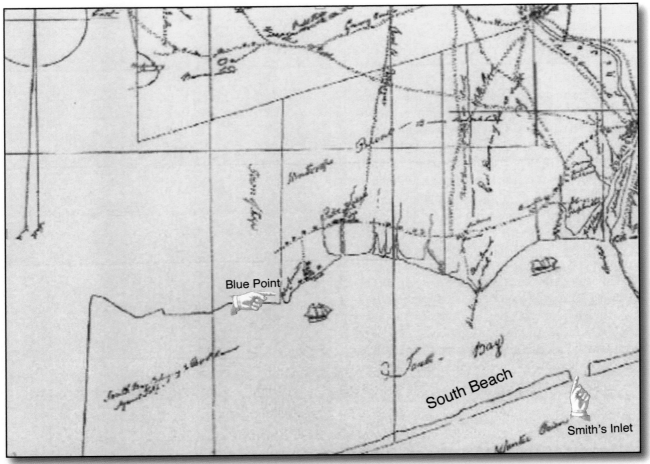

Blue Point

South Beach

Smith's Inlet

Isaac Hulse
1749 - 1807

*D*rawn by cartographer Isaac Hulse in 1797, above is a map of the town of Brookhaven in the County of Suffolk. It was made from an actual survey of the outlines of said town in October and November of 1737. The east line of said town was run south in the year 1792 and included the barrier beach showing Smith's Inlet or New Inlet.

The detailed map of 1792 was included with other town surveys as directed by Simeon De Witt, Surveyor General of the State of New York. Abutting the Hulse survey was the Samuel Wheeler survey of Islip Town. Both were included in the New York State map by Simeon DeWitt in the year 1802 to form the first official map of the state of New York.

"Said map was laid down by the Magnetic Meridian line as the needlepoint at present." In other words, it was based on the magnetic declination existing in 1797, the date of the map, or one hundred years after the date of the Nicoll Patent of Islip Town in 1697. It is today incompetent as evidence of its easterly line in a court of law. The field notes of Isaac Hulse show a discrepancy in distance, indicating he was off by as much as 1290 feet in areas of the survey.

The adjoining Wheeler survey of Islip Town indicates by arrows on the right-hand side, there of true north and magnetic north, the latter being indicated as north by the needle having three degrees of variation. The Wheeler map does nothing more than perpetuate the error contained in the Brookhaven or Hulse map in locating the Townline because of the current magnetic declination of three degrees west.

Neither map is therefore competent proof in a court of law of the existence of the east line of the Nicoll Patent as it existed in 1697.

Simeon De Witt Map 1802
Geographer and Surveyor

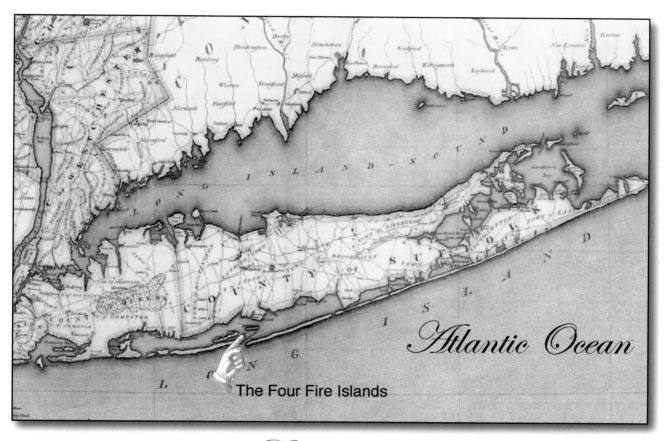

Atlantic Ocean

The Four Fire Islands

1756 - 1834

Simeon De Witt Esq.
Surveyor General
State of New York

eWitt was a geographer and surveyor general of the Continental Army during the American Revolution and surveyor general of the State of New York for fifty years from 1784 until his death.

In 1802, DeWitt produced a detailed map of the state of New York, which was engraved by Gideon Fairman. The map is said by historian Gerard Koeppel to have been meticulously drawn and to have set a standard for American cartography. It is still considered the most important map ever made of the Empire State. This map was produced by local surveys and military maps that were in the possession of De-Witt from the Revolutionary War. He also used the Islip map of the barrier beach drawn by Samuel Wheeler in the year 1798. Take note of the four islands called Fire Islands in the Great South Bay. He also utilized the1797 map of the town of Brookhaven by Isaac Halls surveyor of Brookhaven town. De Witt's map was first published in 1802, then in reduced scale in 1804. This map would serve for decades as the state map displayed most commonly in public buildings and private homes. It was admired not only for scientific accuracy, but also for its vision of the state reinventing itself.

DeWitt was appointed New York State survey general in 1784, with New York being one of the few states at that time having such an office. DeWitt died fifty years later still holding that position, having been reappointed and reelected several times.

Strange Separation of Brookhaven Town From Islip Town

Historic map of Suffolk County 1915. Published by E. Belcher Hyde.

The track on the barrier beach between Brookhaven, Islip and Huntington had for many years been in controversy. The western boundary of the jurisdiction of Brookhaven over the South Bay was settled December 15, 1834, by a commission composed of Nathaniel Potter, Joel Jarvis and Selah Carl of Huntington; Elihphalet Smith, Treadwell Scudder and Richard A. Udall, of Islip, and Mordechai Homan, Davis Norton and James M. Fanning of Brookhaven. They decided in their infinite wisdom that the line in question should run from the "northernmost range pole on the South Beach" a due north course "polar direction," across the South Bay to a point on the mainland, which should be marked by a stone monument. Stone monuments were set up at either end of the line on September 15, 1835. The outer end of this line is about four miles east of Fire Island Lighthouse, and the inner end is at the east side of the mouth of the Great River in Islip.

Today these lines make very little sense when you consider that the Pines, Cherry Grove, Sunken Forest, Point O' Woods and Ocean Bay Park and the two most easterly walks in Seaview. Ironically the tax base and zoning are under the jurisdiction of Brookhaven Town. Salt hay was an important commodity for the farmers in the Township of Brookhaven and the barrier beach did not seem to have much significance for the residents of Islip Township. This may have been a reason for the strange separation between the two towns.

Harvesting salt hay, 1800s on the barrier beach, an important commodity for the livestock.

Map of Raccoon Beach
Fire Island 1825

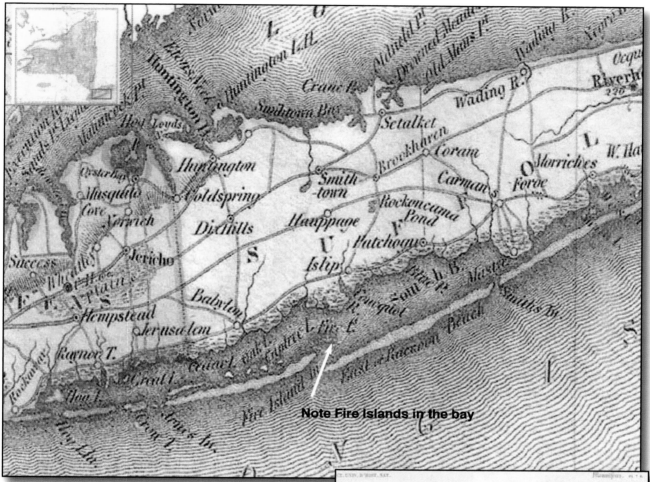

Note Fire Islands in the bay

reated by American cartographer H.S. Tanner, born in New York City, Tanner's Map of North America, was constructed according to the latest information in 1825. Published in Philadelphia, it was one of the most detailed maps of Long Island and the barrier beach for its time.

One of the remarkable things about Tanner's map is that it shows the barrier beach as Raccoon Beach and East Beach, which were early names given for what is now known as Fire Island. It gives credence to the Samuel

**Henry S. Tanner
1786 to 1858**

Wheeler map of 1798 of Islip, where he referred to the barrier beach as East Beach.

From the 1800s to the 1840s, the name Raccoon Beach enjoyed a vogue, as hunting was a popular use for the beach. Douglas Tuomey a frequent contributor to the Long Island Forum, narrated the arrival of a father and son on a raccoon hunting expedition along the barrier beach in one of his stories.

1826 Fire Island Lighthouse

*B*ecause of the great need for a lighthouse on Long Island, President George Washington signed an order for the establishment of the lighthouse at Montauk Point in 1795. Montauk Lighthouse was a giant step forward, but only the partial problem in navigation along the South Shore of Long Island. Ship owners clamored for light at the Fire Island Inlet to mark treacherous waterways into the Great South Bay and also to provide a haven during bad weather for ships. Fire Island Inlet was about midway down Long Island from Montauk to Sandy Hook Light. On March 3, 1825, Congress appropriated money for the purchase of land on the westerly end of the barrier beach, and for the original Fire Island Lighthouse. An amount of $10,000 was secured.

In the progression of the barrier beach a lighthouse was built in 1826 between the Great South Bay and Atlantic Ocean. It would also serve to mark shoals approximately one quarter to one mile offshore of shipping lanes navigating into New York Bay. Fire Island Lighthouse was also a beacon to help ships and other vessels that were making their way through the Fire Island Inlet, north towards the Long Island communities situated on the bay. Fire Island lighthouse was built a stone's throw away from the inlet at the west end of South Beach or today's Fire Island.

Until August, 1891, the color of the tower was yellow or cream color, but at that time was changed to alternate bands of black and white, each band being about 35 feet wide.

The *American Monthly Magazine*, dated 1835 has one of the most visual accounts written about the lighthouse and traversing towards it:

"We have crossed the bay, skirting by the Fire Islands, leaving them a few hundred yards behind us to the north, and have rested our prow upon the classical sands of Raccoon Beach."

"Upon our arrival here, we put in alongside of the new wharf of the eximious Mr. Smith, a person of little importance, being a man under authority, having a wife over him, a keeper of their majesties, the people's lighthouse, adjoining his own tenement, duly appointed and commissioned, a lawful voter, a licensed vendor of "spurrets and things accorden," and the only householder upon the island's ridge."

"Mr. Smith had the happiness in early life, of being blest with parents of taste, in matters of nomenclature, singularly coincident with that of my own. His Christian name was Jeremiah, to; and (perhaps, because his surname was unusual, and difficult to pronounce) his friends and visitors always gave him their greeting, by the gentle and euphonious appellation of "Jerry."

Two things that should be brought to the reader's attention are that the locals referred to Fire Island in that era as Raccoon Beach, the other is that Jeremiah Smith's home was well west of Cherry Grove, and legend has it that he was the first to sell the property now known as the Grove to Archer and Elizabeth Perkinson. Archer and Elizabeth Perkinson started their restaurant in 1868, after the great partition of 1878. The Perkinsons' purchased property, and built a two-story hotel, however history has shown it was not Jeremiah Smith.

It was only natural to name the lighthouse after a geographical location called Fire Island Inlet, even though some of the locals referred to the location as Raccoon Beach. Today instead of having the Raccoon Lighthouse, it was properly named the Fire Island Lighthouse.

On March 3, 1857 Congress appropriated $40,000 for a new lighthouse. A site 200-feet northeast of the 1826 tower was chosen, and construction began that summer under the direction of Lieutenant J. C. Duane of the Army Corps of Engineers. Due to the island's elevation, the entire station would be built upon a one-hundred-foot terrace. Acording to an entry in an 1858 report to the lighthouse board, bricks from the old tower and dwelling were used to finish the terrace that surrounds the entire station.

By June 1891, in a monthly report to the lighthouse board, it was noted that the outside of the tower needed paint or wash to protect it from deterioration. Plans were made to give the tower a new distinct day mark and by August of that year, materials had been delivered to the site and workers had begun applying it. By September the lighthouse had received its unique black-and-white alternating bands, a scheme it still has today.

Lightship Station 1896

One part of Fire Island history that is often ignored is the impact of lightships. These manned buoys played an important role in our lighthouse legacy, and duty on board them was generally tougher than that at the lighthouse. Harsh weather, remoteness, loneliness and collision with ships were some of the unsavory aspects of life aboard a lightship. The lightship station was established in 1896, and the first light vessel stationed off Fire Island was LV 58. Prior to its Fire Island duty, it had been stationed at Nantucket Shoals from 1894 to 1896. LV 58 left Fire Island in 1897, and became a relief vessel in Massachusetts until being sunk by a storm on December 10, 1905.

Light Vessel (LV) 68 was ordered built, to be stationed off Fire Island; $80,000 was appropriated for the project. It

Fire Island Light Vessel No. 68 moored in 96-feet of water, 9.8 miles 8 1/16 West from Fire Island Lighthouse N.Y.

was also rigged for sail and was equipped for fog with a steam chime whistle and a hand-operated 1,000-pound bell.

While LV 68 was moored off island, it was twice hit by ships, on May 8, 1916, the *S.S. Philadelphian* rammed it, and on March 30, 1924, the English steamship *Castilian* struck the lightship on her port quarter. She was saved from floundering only by the prompt action of the crew, which partly plugged the big gap in her side with planks and tarpaulins. She was then towed to Staten Island by the lighthouse tender for repairs.

Painters worked all night on a new vessel that had been built to serve on the Phantom Bank off Virginia. Painted a brilliant light red, she proceeded to the Fire Island post and initiated for regular light ship duty until LV 68 was put back in service. Many Fire Islanders knew the lightship from a flashing light in her vicinity on the ocean. Others remember her during the days of rum row, when the big rum-running fleet was captured by the Coast Guard patrolling the islands inlet and offshore waters.

During the Second World War LV 68 was replaced by lightship No. 114. This ship served as the Fire Island Lightship until 1942 and was armed for wartime service with a single six-pound gun and placed into service as an examination vessel at Bayshore, New York. Her log reports illustrate how real threats to shipping on the East Coast were, as her log for Christmas Day 1941 mentions flares from a German U. boat off the Fire Island Inlet.

Fire Island's lightship station was unmarked from 1942 to 1945. A whistling buoy equipped with a powerful light showing a 1,100 candlepower prism was then stationed at a position of the old lightships. The whistling buoy anchored in ninety-six-feet of water is no longer there. However, the history of the old lightships that were stationed approximately forty miles east of the entrance to New York Harbor still linger on in the annals of Fire Island history.

Ferdinand Rudolf Hassler
Early Illustrations of Fire Island

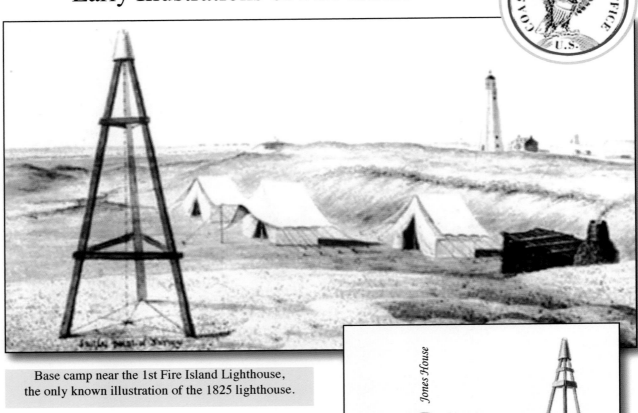

Base camp near the 1st Fire Island Lighthouse, the only known illustration of the 1825 lighthouse.

Dragging the famous carriage along the beach.

Jones House

A 200 pound theodolite, note in the background is the Jones house.

The illustrations believed to be drawn by Hassler's engineers, who worked for him as surveyors, show the earliest known images of Fire Island, including the lighthouse, which was built just seven years prior. The illustration's show what the camp of his survey field party looked like in the 1830s. In the illustration, Ferdinand Hassler's 200-pound, 24-inch field theodolite sits in a tent protected from the elements. Also visible is a dispassionately designed and reinforced field carriage. The carriage Hassler used to carry heavy surveying equipment his books and maps, also contained a warming chamber and disappearing dining table. Life on the barrier beach was evidently not all hardship. In writings of the time, it is noted the carriage always attracted a great deal of attention wherever it went.

Ferdinand Rudolf Hassler 1834
Survey of the Coast & Map

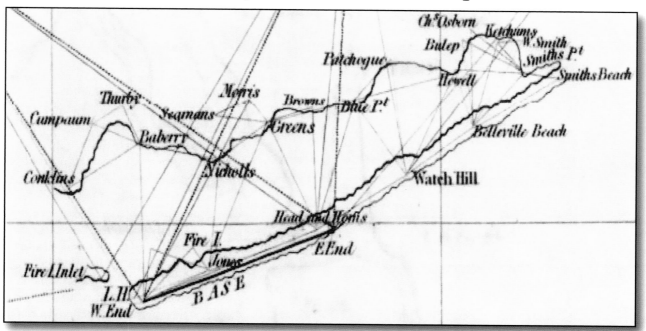

Ferdinand Rudolf Hassler
1772 - 1843

*S*wiss-born, American geodesist, mathematician and surveyor, Ferdinand Hassler was superintendent of the United States Coast Survey and the Bureau of Weights and Measures. He established a baseline on Fire Island that was utilized to survey other coastal and inland areas. Surveys included the lighthouse, Jones's house, and the Fire Island Inlet. His map was the first map to call the barrier beach Fire Island.

Army and Navy Chronicle 1834 Survey of the Coast
Third Report of Mr. Hassler:

"Report of draft of Hassler, as Superintendent of the survey of the coast additional to the dated May 17, 1834 contained an account of the progress of that work during the summer and until November 1834."

"I also stated in that report from the observations upon the stations of Rulens and Westhills, upon Long Island, there appeared to be sent itself the prospect of the baseline far more advantageous, in every point of view than that measured preliminary in English neighborhood, New Jersey, namely upon a beach called Fire Island Beach, upon the South Shore of Long Island, which separates what is called the great South Beach from the ocean."

"I directed then all the assistance, not otherwise especially engaged, the men and apparatus, and equipment, to the Fire Island Lighthouse, in the neighborhood of which the west end of the baseline was to fall; and directed the assistance joining there, to make a detailed survey of the beach from its West End and, to Head and Horns head, and even Watch Hill."

"It is my intention to have the typography of the south part of Long Island near the baseline fully executed this fall, as well upon the land as for the soundings of the South Bay, that lies between Fire Island Beach and the main shore of the island."

Controversy Over Name Change

Not all the citizens were happy with the name change of South Beach to Fire Island; much controversy took place amongst the citizens. Here is a letter to the local newspaper strongly protesting this act.

The Patchogue Advance
November 26, 1956
By Osborne Shaw:

Within the last few years there has developed a growing tendency to refer to the Great South Beach within the boundaries of the town of Brookhaven as Fire Island. This has been due to the carelessness to new arrivals and non-residents who would have extended the term, Fire Island eastward from that part of the barrier beach in the town of Islip into the town of Brookhaven and now refer to the whole of the beach east of Fire Island Inlet as Fire Island and sometimes simply as The Island. It is a confusing, misleading and erroneous habit and is entirely at variance with all deeds, records and maps.

Nathaniel R. Howell in his history of the Town of Islip printed in Bailey's book, "Long Island a History of Two Great Counties Nassau and Suffolk" (1949), Volume 1 page 326, states "To the native, only that part of the beach from the State Park westward to the inlet is Fire Island.

The early Brookhaven Town records always speak of the beach as the South Beach and is so designated by Isaac Hulse in his survey of the town of Brookhaven made in 1797. In the Atlas of 1839, map 5 of Suffolk County names it Great South Beach. It is the earliest reference I have seen by that name. By 1873 Fire Island Beach had come into use along with great South Beach and is so shown in the "Atlas of Long Island" published that year by Beers, Comstock and Cline.

Richard M. Bayles, a native of Middle Island, historian and surveyor, in his "Historical and Descriptive Sketches of Suffolk County" published in 1874 makes

no mention whatsoever of Fire Island Beach but does have the following to say in his chapter on the Town of Islip, page 198: "The Great South Beach" opposite this town, as far west as the Connetquot River, belongs to Brookhaven Town.

It is only in very recent times that the term "Fire Island" has been applied to the Great South Beach. Not until after the First World War, when new men in the Coast Guard, mostly Southerners were sent to man the Coast Guard stations along our coast, did "Fire Island" (without beach) come into use.

The following entry found in the Brookhaven Town Trustees' records, June 1932 - October 1936, on page 350 under date of Dec. 1935 it reads:

"The Town Clerk presented for the consideration of the Trustees a questionnaire received from the Bureau of Geographic Names, Department of the Interior, Washington, D. C., requesting information concerning the proper name of the barrier beach in the southern part of the town, whether known as "Great South Beach" or "Fire Island Beach."

The matter was discussed at length, Trustee Rogers examining the records in the matter. It was considered by members to be desirable to continue the name, "South Beach or Fire Island Beach." For geographic reference purposes, the beach having been referred to by the name in all the older [sic] Town Records. The clerk was instructed to so advise the department.

I wrote to Mr. James E. Tooker, the former longtime Town Clerk of the town of Babylon and now that town's well-informed town historian and I quote in part from his reply dated 17th of September, 1956. "All my life for most of it I have lived within sight of Fire Island Lighthouse. In the 1890s our folks would often go to the ocean in summer, I always understood then that Fire Island referred to the area in the vicinity of the lighthouse.In view of all the foregoing facts, I failed to see any authority or reason of mentioning the barrier beach anywhere in the Town of Brookhaven by any other name than South Beach."

54

Fire Island or Great South Beach 1873
Published by Beers, Comstock and Clein

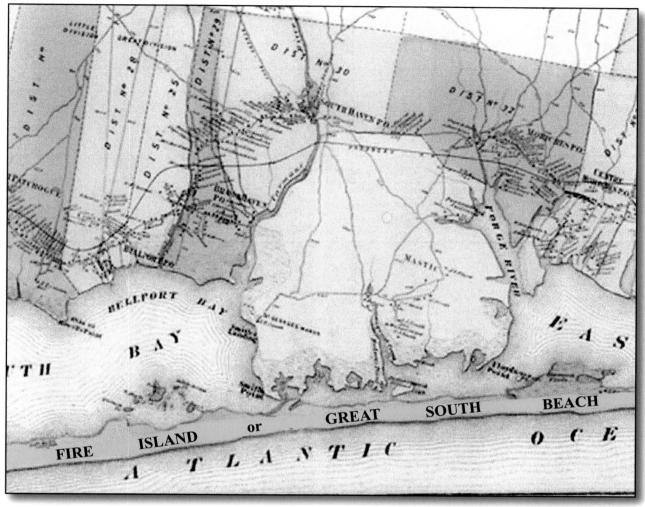

This Atlas was published in 1873, showing Fire Island and the Great South Beach and East Beach. It was originally created to visualize land boundaries of Islip and Brookhaven to determine property taxes. This ambitious project became the first comprehensive Atlas of Long Island. It shows the division of Islip Town, referring to the west end as Fire Island, while Brookhaven maintained the position that it was the Great South Beach.

F. W. Beers came from a family of publishers. While in school, Frederick, his cousin Silas N. Beers and their friend D. Jackson Lake, studied under the mapmaker J. H.

**Frederick W. Beers
1839 - 1933**

French, at Newtown Academy, Newtown, Connecticut. When French left the Academy in 1855 to pursue a position with the New York State mapping project he took his three former students along as associates. The project, said to be notable mapmaking accomplishments of any state at that time, and was a training ground for the mapmakers.

Islip's position followed the Surf Hotel and Sammis making himself the Fire Island postmaster. The Surf Hotel's office address and also the Fire Island Lighthouse used this post office within the Surf Hotel. Ferdinand Rudolph Hassler's survey of the coast and map of 1834 was the first to utilize the name "Fire Island Beach." The second was the Beers, Comstock and Clein Atlas of Long Island. Additionally, other commercial enterprises started to follow on the west end of the barrier beach establishing the name "Fire Island."

Sea Shore Attractions 1890s

*R*eprinted from *Yesteryear in Bayshore 1892* with corrections as needed:

"The bay makes deep indentations, making favorable coves and harbors for anchoring crafts of all kinds. There are numerous fishing boats and pleasure yachts constantly afloat. The crab fishing in these inlets is a great attraction to many visitors, especially of the juvenile order. Some crabs, both hard and soft shell, can also be ensnared with good success burrowing along the shores of the inlets.

A more generally popular and even more poetic amusement is blue fishing beyond Fire Island. This is one of the most important industries and thousands of these deep-sea beauties are shipped from here each week during the entire season. A start is made early in the morning and the rundown to Fire Island takes, with a favorable wind, less than two hours. Skimming steadily along under half reefed sail, the boats glide back-and-forth over the familiar spots where the fish usually resort. According to the run, anywhere from five to fifty can be count on a day's trip, landing back at the mainland again in the afternoon. There is also fine weak fish and seabass which can be taken along the shore and the outer bay.

It is hardly necessary to say that no visitor should fail to take the boat trips to Fire Island to this interesting and celebrated spot. Its claims upon the attention of tourist are many, and have long been recognized. The very situation of the barrier beach on the verge of the great Atlantic, the last outpost of the Western Continent gives a distinct and romantic impression. This is augmented by the long sandy beaches and reefs, being a simple and veritable offspring of the sea.

The Fire Island Light, as is well known, is last cited by the outgoing steamers, as well as the first glimpse of home court by the inward bound. The central point of interest on the Island is the great Surf Hotel with immense accommodations, having room for over a thousand people. This was purchased by the State Government in 1892, but has been used only once hitherto, and has not proved to any such extent as was expected a detriment to the shore.

All who are acquainted with the real facts in the case, (cholera epidemic of 1892) and not simply with exaggerated and inaccurate accounts in some of the newspapers, that the people maintained merely their uncontested rights with quiet and unvarying dignity. There was never any need for excitement here in some sections. The entire affair was a good illustration of how imaginative and sensational journalism can doctor up when they make a brilliant effort in that direction.

There are several other interesting buildings upon Fire Island beside the Surf Hotel, as well as a Life Saving Station, of which Capt. Charles E. Weeks has charge. Probably no point on the shore has witnessed more noteworthy wrecks than this station. During the storming periods, the heroic men at this post have a great deal on their hands, and are constantly on alert. The equipment of this station is very complete and will prove interesting to every observer whether he has been in a severe storm are not.

The same is true of the Life Saving Station, known as the "Point of the Wood," under the able charge of Capt. William H. Miller. The superintendent of the Lighthouse in this part of the shore is entrusted to Mr. Arthur Dorminy.

At Fire Island, there is also good surf bathing during the season. The island is a favorite resort for picnics and excursion parties which go to spend the day and enjoy the famous fish dinners which are here prepared in special form."

Ocean and bay off Fire Island contributed to tourism, fishing, clamming and the oyster industry in the 1890s.

David Sturges S. S. Sammis 1856

*I*n 1856, Fire Island's name became standard on the west end of the barrier beach. David Sammis was a promoter and the first Fire Island postmaster.

The Surf Hotel, which was located just east of the Fire Island Lighthouse was an expansive building built on 120 acres of land that David Sammis owned, or so he thought. A battle over the ownership of this land went on for years with Sammis winning. Sammis built the hotel in 1856 and by 1880 the hotel boasted rooms for 1500 guests.

Birdseye view of the Sammis Hotel, note the steamboat and the Fire Island Lighthouse.

Sammis created the first Fire Island Post Office going by that name, serving as the first postmaster on Fire Island. The lighthouse also utilized the Sammis Fire Island post office, as did his guests when in summer season and the Surf Hotel advertised itself as located on Fire Island. By general consent and custom it was called by that name until by right of adverse possession it was clearly entitled to the designation.

David Sturges S.S. Sammis, a man of immense ego, was born in the town of Huntington, near Babylon in 1818. In the year 1835 he went to New York to learn the druggist business. There he stayed for two years, but the peculiar atmosphere did not agree with him. In 1848 he leased the property on the corner of East Broadway and Pike Street where he opened a hotel under the name of East Broadway House, which was recognized as a headquarters for politicians without regard to party.

In 1855 he bought an undivided portion of Fire Island, which had been used only as pasture for cattle. The next year he built a hotel with accommodations for one hundred guests on his recent land investment. Under his skillful and liberal management, this hotel immediately became popular, also proving a success financially. During the fol-

David S. S. Sammis
1818 to 1895

lowing winter, Sammis added one hundred feet to his building, making everything first-class, to the extent of introducing gas lighting throughout the whole hotel.

In 1858 he sold East Broadway House and devoted his entire time to his real estate ventures and the Surf Hotel. A $25,000 steamboat, built to carry his passengers across the Great South Bay, was caught in a squall one winter night and utterly ruined. The next spring, with his accustomed energy, Mr. Sammis replaced the wrecked ferry with a better one. To further add to the comfort of his visitors to Fire Island, he built a street trolley from the train depot in the Village of Babylon to his steamboat landing on the bay.

On the top of the Surf Hotel a cupola was built for telegraph observations of vessels heading to Manhattan. It became so advantageous to the Surf Hotel customers that Western Union constructed a marine observatory a short distance from the hotel and lighthouse. This observatory would notify shipping lines that were heading westward to facilitate accommodations in Manhattan of their arrival. It was a plain square structure, solidly built with heavy timbers securely braced with guy wires at each corner, fastened to heavy anchors in the beach sand. Two lower stories were used as a dwelling by observer Peter Keegan and his family. The square upper room sixty-feet from the ground commanded an extensive view in all directions (see page 72).

David Sammis sold his hotel property to New York State in 1892 to be used for a cholera quarantine station.

Fire Island Relief Huts
Circa 1850s

One of the early movements utilizing the name Fire Island can be recorded by "The American Humane Relief Society," founded in New York City by a group of philanthropists in the early 1800s. Its purpose was to find some means of aiding shipwrecked sailors whose own existence relied on some sort of humanitarian help while stranded on Fire Island.

The savage storms that ravished the coast of Long Island in the 1800s resulted in shipwrecks of various tonnage and an undetermined number of lives were lost. The word of the disasters coming year after year of shipwrecks now gradually drew public attention.

All along abandoned stretches of Fire Island Beach, the society erected at several-mile intervals, small compact and sturdy huts known as humane relief houses. They were smaller than a present-day one car garage, unfurnished as far as any pretense of comfort goes, but held the essentials of shelter, warmth, water and fuel. The doors were unlocked with no apparent latches. In each hut there was a small cast iron wood-burning stove and a good supply of kindling with matches and a large lantern. There was also a large keg of fresh water, tins of ship's biscuits and a canister of tea. It was a spartan diet, but enough to sustain life and revive half-drowned or frozen souls who managed to stagger into them. A sign was on the inside of the door, printed in several languages, (English, French, German, Portuguese and Spanish), giving directions and the best means of obtaining further assistance. Posts were also set up at short intervals along the dunes with arrows pointing to the nearest relief hut.

This crude sensible provision accounted for the saving of many a life in years before the United States Life-Saving Stations were spread along the shores of Fire Island. Notwithstanding of efforts of the society, there were as usual, those who took advantage of unprotected property. The American Humane Relief Society appointed a keeper for each house. Unfortunately, the keeper usually lived on the mainland across the bay, visiting the shelter only occasionally to see that it was properly provisioned. Frequently they found them stripped of their provisions and even the small wood-burning stoves. In one unfortunate case, the keeper after being kept from his usual inspection by a heavy snowstorm and ice flow, found the door of one hut open and banging in the winter wind. There stretched on the floor were two frozen corpses. Nevertheless, many a fugitive from the surf owed their lives to these relief huts well before life-saving crews were formed to patrol the barrier beach in winter.

Today there is not the slightest trace of any Humane Relief Huts. The important part of the story is that the name Fire Island started to progress with the public from the West End of the beach.

Relief hut.
Sketch by Douglas Tuomey

Fire Island Lifesaving Station 1878

The Fire Island Life Saving Station was the most westerly station placed on a land parcel acquired by the federal government in 1825 for the construction of the lighthouse. Situated on the east side of Fire Island Inlet, the Life Saving Station was built around 1878. Prior to this, a volunteer Life Saving Station manned by volunteers was built in 1849 to aid shipwrecks and sailors in distress.

Initially maned by a keeper and six surfmen, a seventh surfmen was added for winter months. One surfman maintained a lookout watch during daylight hours from the watchtower constructed on the roof top of each station. Spacing of the stations along the barrier beach allowed for visual surveillance of the entire coast during daylight hours. In non-daylight hours surfmen took turns walking a beach patrol with one surfman going in each direction from the station. They were required to meet fellow patrolmen from the next station to exchange copper disks before returning to their home station where the keepers recorded their trips in a log. If trouble was found, they quickly returned to the station and advised the keeper of the circumstances or lit a Coston flare. Keepers then organized the crew for rescue or aid for whatever unimaginable crises ensued.

USLSS Coston flare.

In addition to the basic equipment necessary for saving lives, there were other technological developments in the USLSS (United States Lifesaving Service). Carts pulled by men or horses, were used to bring equipment to the scene of a wreck. Every surfman was equipped with Coston flares on his nightly patrol to warn ships away or to summon additional help. By 1889 all the stations from Forge River and the most easterly to the most westerly Fire Island Station were linked by telegraph, which allowed for instant communication and other major rescue operations. This enabled the effort of more than one station to assist in any hazard taking place.

Going from east to west there were seven stations on the barrier beach starting with Forge River, Smith Point, Bellport, Blue Point, Lone Hill, Point O' Woods and Fire Island.

As an economic move, U. S. Congress merged the U. S. Revenue Cutter Service with the U. S. Life-Saving Service to form the present-day Coast Guard. This act to create the Coast Guard was approved on January 20, 1915 as a separate agency. The only active rescue service left on the barrier beach is the Fire Island Coast Guard station situated basically in the same location as its predecessor. The Fire Island Lifesaving Station, in its day, guarded and protected the surrounding area, including the Great South Bay and Atlantic Ocean.

Life Saving Stations on Fire Island

Lone Hill (Pines) Great South Beach April 9, 1911
Ship stranded on the bar. Station number 23 –
opened 1855 closed 1946

Shooting the life line U.S. Life Saving Station
Fire Island circa 1900 - Station number 25 -
opened 1849 still active as Coast Guard Station.

U.S. Life Saving Station Point O' Woods
circa 1900 with crew. Station number 24 –
opened 1856 closed 1937

Life Boat afloat U.S. Life Saving Station
Bellport circa 1900 - station number 21 -
opened 1879 closed 1951

Return of the Life Boat U.S. Life Saving Station
Blue Point Beach circa 1900 – Station number 22 –
opened 1856 closed 1946

Breeches Buoy in Action U.S. Life Saving Station
Smith Point circa 1900 – Station number 20 –
opened 1872 closed 1937

Forge River Life Saving Station #19, see images on page 72.

History of Fire Island State Park

Although the fact that the Fire Island State Park was older by nearly twenty years than any other state park on Long Island, its historical background is probably least known. Lack of knowledge about Fire Island State Park is due to its early inaccessibility and not because its history has been uneventful. Originally known as Fire Island State Park, established in 1908, it was the first state park on Long Island and established its presence on Fire Island in 1892. Having done so, the state continued the progression of the name "Fire Island" on the west end of the barrier beach.

In 1892, the port of New York became frazzled over a cholera scare. Strict watch was held on vessels with incoming immigrants and passengers from foreign countries. On August 30, 1892, a ship arrived in New York Harbor from Hamburg loaded with passengers and because of the scare, the ship was forced to remain in quarantine. Several other ships were held up and due to the congestion in the harbor, health authorities were forced to pursue an isolated spot to hold passengers of these boats. Even though some were not infected with cholera, they might have been exposed to the disease.

To meet the need of the Board of Health in both city and state, immediate purchase of the Surf hotel on Fire Island as the most rational location for a quarantine station was demanded. Governor Rosewell P. Flower ordered the purchase of the property and gave his personal check in the amount of $50,000 as a partial payment on the purchase price of $210,000 for the hotel including about 129 acres of land, dock and incidental buildings on Fire Island. Also included in this purchase was the dock at the foot of Fire Island Avenue in Babylon.

An organized demonstration of fishermen and residents from Islip and Babylon amassed at the dock to prevent a steamship called the *Cephus* crowded with quarantine passengers to dock. News of these activities was sent to New York by telegraph. Soon several companies of the 69th Regiment, New York National Guard, and one company from the 13th Regiment, arrived in Babylon together with a unit of field artillery. At Fire Island a boat with one battalion of Naval Reservist ready for riot duty took possession of the property. Federalized troops left Fire Island on October 5, but for the duration of the quarantine two deputy sheriff's were stationed at the Babylon dock.

By summer of 1893 the cholera scare had completely subsided. In the following spring the state legislature by chapter 357 of the laws of 1894 authorized the Department of Health to lease the Fire Island buildings for hotel purposes. Thus, it was that ill wind of the plague threatening New York City that brought about establishment of the first state park on Long Island, and the only ocean front park in the entire state until the opening of Jones Beach State Park in 1920 by Robert Moses.

In cooperation with Commissioner Moses, the New York City Rotary Club in 1926 created a crippled boys' camp. The camp, known as Camp Cheerful, consisted of nine cabins, an administration building, storehouse, infirmary, mess hall, helpers' quarters, water supply and equipment. On September 21, 1938, the now famous 1938 hurricane hit Fire Island with high tides and fury, destroying all developed sections of the park just east of the lighthouse. When the storm subsided, there was nothing but wreckage. Camp Cheerful, which had been closed for the season had completely disappeared. The Western Union building, which had stood for over fifty years, was dessimated, except several hundred feet away from the building's foundation, two stories of the old watchtower could be seen.

From this unsettled establishment, the state transformed their Fire Island properties into park land. In 1924 Robert Moses, who was appointed commissioner of Long Island Parks, amended the boundary to include lands built westward from the oceans, which forms the outline of the Fire Island State Park, as we know it today.

West Island or West Fire Island - East Island or East Fire Island

here has been much controversy, and mis-interpretation by historians about two islands located on the Great South Bay, five miles southeast of Bay Shore and one-mile northeast of the Fire Island Lighthouse. At one time these islands were part of the barrier beach and came into being during the great storms of 1690 to 1691, which broke through the very fragile barrier beach and deposited the remaining sand into the Great South Bay.

Historians have argued over how many islands were created from 1690 to 1700. The 1674 map of Robert Ryder shows the barrier beach as a peninsula with no islands in the Great South Bay near southeast Bay Shore. Henry R. Bang, in his book, "The West Fire Island Story" and other historians have made assertions that the Ryder Map illustrates one island, which had broken away from the barrier strip. Unfortunately, if one looks at the location of this inlet island, due north are the Hempstead Plaines, this would take the location somewhere into Nassau County, keeping in mind that during the Revolutionary War, the Inlet is shown to be in the vicinity west of what is known today as Point O' Woods, (see opposite page for conformation).

The Thomas Jefferys map of 1755 shows the same inlet south of the Hempstead Plains with no island. Agent John Andre's Spy Map 1781 locates Fire Island north of the barrier beach. North of the inlet, he refers to as the Blue Point Inlet and makes no mention the number of islands in that vicinity. John Wheeler's map of 1798 shows four islands and lists them as Fire Island as does the Simon Dewitt map of 1802. A Beers and Comstock Atlas of 1873 shows Fire Island as Three Islands. No map, survey, nautical charts or town maps of the 1860s show more than four Fire Islands in the Great South Bay.

West Island is on the left and East Island is on the right, circa 1920s.

Numerous names have been given to these Islands: Fire Islands, West Fire Island, East Fire Island, West Island, East Island, Thompson's Island, Holland's Island, and Beacon Fire Island. Another theory is given by Douglas Tuomey, quoting from the "Long Island Forum" in March 1959, a much respected and admired historian, "In evidence a half-century ago, was to the effect about 1770 then Royal Governor of New York, tiring of the loss of ships and men along the outer beach, made a contract with a local indian tribe to light fires on the islands inside the inlet, in order to guide ships into the safer waters of the bay."

In 1901 Frank Buchacek, proprietor of Islip's Orowoc Hotel purchased some acres on West Island to build a modern summer hotel and resort. A large pier was to be built for boat landings as well as a two-story building with an elaborate dining hall, café, and kitchen. There is absolutely no evidence that this hotel was ever built. However, in 1922 during the Roaring 20s, a group of local businessmen with Edward Thompson as the head, created a development company including Dr. George King, Selah Clock and Edward Lyons. A great deal of money was spent building bulkheads, docks and artesian wells. Miles of boardwalks were built that crisscrossed the island which is only a half-mile long and a quarter of a mile wide. A twenty-room hotel called the Casino with approximately ten summer cottages was also built for renters.

The depression ended the developers' dreams and many families left. The hurricanes came, and the Casino, the pier, and many of the cottages were destroyed. What was left of the Casino was finally demolished in the late 1950s. Thus, came the end of an era when Congress passed a law in 1964 with the establishment of the Fire Island National Seashore which acquired the islands.

Difference Over the Name
West Fire Island or West Island

Patchogue Advance,
July 22, 1927

"In another column is printed an indignant letter from Dr. George S. King, the famous Bay Shore surgeon and head of King's Private Hospital, against the use of the name "West Island" in describing Little Fire Island or Thompson's Island, as it has been most generally known for the last twelve or fifteen years. The doctor vigorously declares that this island is the only original blown in the bottle Fire Island, and that to change the name to West Island is little short of desecration.

We are not so sure of that. Before us is an official government map issued by the Coast and Geodetic Survey in Washington, on which the island is called West Fire Island, to distinguish it from East Fire Island, otherwise and by far more popularly known as Hollands Island. If this map is correct, Messrs. Gerard and Bell probably did wisely in leaving out the "Fire" and calling their new development West Island. It hardly could be called a manufactured name. Again, with so many "Fire Islands" anchored in and around the edge of The Great South Bay, were not the realtors justified in adapting a name from the government one that would differentiate it from the others?

Maps, however, sometimes make mistakes, and who shall say that the right name of this patch of green in the middle of the bay with so many summer homes will soon be erected? How does an island get its name? It isn't christened like a baby, and there is no official record of any correct name. Its right name is what it is known as, and there are so many conflicting claims and legends for the group of islands in the bay as to make the nomenclature confusing.

We are inclined to believe that Fire Island Beach is called Fire Island much more commonly than Fire Island Beach. The light is certainly the Fire Island Light and not the Fire Island Beach light. Ask one hundred persons at random who come to the beach what its name is, and ninety will tell you "Fire Island." If popular terminology means anything, the patrons of Sammis's old Surf Hotel would have told you, after a visit that they had been on Fire Island. The name of the place in our estimation, is what the greatest number of people call it.

We have the greatest respect for Dr. King and his intimate knowledge of the bay and beach, but we do not think Messrs. Gerard and Bell made an egregious blunder in naming their development, Beacon, "Fire Island."

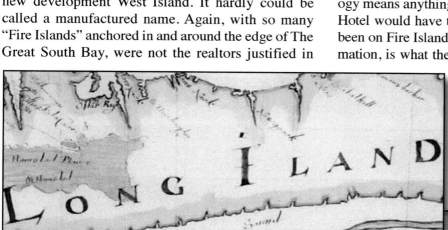

Ryder map of 1674

Not Fire Island Inlet

There is controversy by historians as to whether this island south of the Hempstead plains could possibly be West or East Fire Island. This is a misconception since the island is too far west from the inlet south of Bay Shore.

Fire Island Inlet

Turn of the Century Docks

White House & Pavilon at Water Isl., 1905

Dock at Smith Point Landing, 1908

Dock on the Bay at Saltaire, 1907

Point 'O Woods Dock, 1905

Fire Island State Park Landing, 1919

Ocean Beach Dock, 1910

Summary

Breakers at Ocean Beach early 1900s

These historical happenings countless years ago naming the barrier beach led to some remarkable actions many years later. Though the interest in the story has waxed and waned through the years, it can now be told, perhaps in part thanks to the original newfound spy map of Major John Andre and the British Army utilizing Fire Island West as a beacon for ships to navigate on the Great South Bay. Dispatches during the revolution to headquarters in Manhattan from Long Island, confirm that the term Fire Island was utilized long before historians commented in their erroneous facts in the naming of Fire Island.

These legends fall naturally into three classes. The first class contains tales that the writer knows to be true because he was there when and as events occurred. The second group of stories he believes to be true because they were told and retold him by upright and honest people whose reputation for veracity have been unimpeachable and who obviously believe the stories themselves. The third class is composed of tales that it seems, are impossible of verification or of refutation.

Steamer on the way to
Cherry Grove, 1890.

The difficulty of confirming some of these stories, is that in 1911 a fire swept through the New York State Library in Albany, destroying crucial records and vital manuscripts, including more than 450,000 books, 270,000 manuscripts, and the entire catalog of almost one million cards. It was truly one of the greatest library disasters in modern times; therefore, one had to look at other verifications on the Fire Island label. The author's research was done by only printed material, verifiable, which was past maps, surveys and nautical charts.

Included are traditional stories of the barrier beach to entertain the reader, otherwise one only had to follow the succession of maps to see how Fire Island's name came about from a progression of events.

This much can be said: "A good portion of past written legends and folklore had no solid basis in fact."

Fire Island: How It Got Its Name by Dates, Surveys and Maps

Cartographer	Date	Names	Maps & Surveys
Adrian Block Map	1614	No mention of the Barrier Beach	Dutch Map (1st map showing Long Island & the New World)
Johanes Van Kuelen Map	1664	Prince Maurits Eyland	Dutch Map
Arendt Roggeveen Map	1675	Prince Maurits Eylant	Dutch Map
John Seller Map	1674	Outline of the Barrier Beach	British Map
John Thorton Map	1685	South Sand Beach	American Map
Robert Ryder	1674	First Survey of the Barrier Beach	American Map
Herman Moll	1708	South Sand Beach	American Map
Thomas Jefferys	1755	South Beach of Sand and Stone	British Map
Major John Andre	1781	First to Record Fire Island on Map	British Spy Map
Samuel Wheeler	1798	Survey of Fire Island and Inlet	Islip Town Survey
Isaac Hulse	1797	Survey of Barrier Beach	Brookhaven Town Survey
Simeon De Witt	1802	Barrier Beach & Long Island	NY State Map
Henry S. Tanner	1825	Raccoon Beach	North American Map
Fire Island Lighthouse	1825	Named after Fire Island Inlet	Geographical location
Ferdinand Hassler	1834	Survey of coast & map, list Barrier Beach as Fire Island	
Frederick W. Beers	1873	Fire Island or Great South Beach	Suffolk County Map
Fire Island Relief Huts	1850	Founded by "The American Humane Relief Society"	
David S. Sammis	1856	Surf Hotel 1st Fire Island Post Office using the name Fire Island	
Fire Island Life Saving Sta.	1878	Named after the physical location of the Lighthouse	
Fire Island State Park	1894	First state park on Long Island with ocean front	
Fire Island Light Ship Station	1896	Continuation of the name Fire Island	
Fire Island National Seashore	1964	Brookhaven renames South Beach to Fire Island	
Fire Island Tide	1977	First News Magazine with complete circulation from Lighthouse to Wilderness Zone & all Communities in between	

There are no maps or surveys showing Five Islands.

Post Cards from the Past

Margaret Fuller Memorial Point O' Woods, 1908.
The first important American feminist book
written in 1845, "Woman in the 19th Century."
See page 18.

Saltaire docks and Great South Bay
looking north,
Circa 1920s.

A group of summer homes
along the boardwalk,
circa 1920s Saltaire.

Fire Island School serving all of the communities.
Corner of Wilmot Road and Midway walk
Ocean Beach circa 1920s.

The Ridge at Point O' Woods 1907.
Many of the homes were destroyed in the
hurricane of 1938.

Western Union Telegraph Tower with the
Fire Island Lighthouse, 1878
now in the vicinity west of Kismet.

Native American Designations on the Barrier Beach

The tendency of the English and Dutch language to reduce many words that have more than one and usually more than three syllables, is exemplified again and again in theses place-names of Indian origin. For instance the familiar name tomahawk (English) is reduced from tu-meltah-who-uk (Algonians). The following pronunciations are found on old maps, deeds and writings from past historians.

1614 – Dutch map of New Netherlands -
Sictem Hackey

1657 – Dutch interpretation of Algonquin names on the Barrier Beach:
Secoutagh
Sichtewach
Sighewach

1668 – Brookhaven Town Records, Vol. 1:
Owenamchog
Onkoue-nameech-quke

1911 – William Tooker -
"Indian Place and Names"
Sichetanyhacky

1896 - Martha Bockee Flint –
"Early Long Island Colonial Study"
Siekrewhacky

Other Early Native Names:
Mattanhbank
Seal Island - Eninashs
Niac
Ahki

Barrier Beach names east of Smith Point,
Found on vintage maps of barrier beach:
Ponquogue
Shinnecock
Wegonthatak
Waspeunk

1918 - James Truslow Adams -
"History of South Hampton":
Kitchaminechoke
Enoughquanauc

Above image engraved on a powder horn of a native south shore indian, 1700s.
In 1524 Florentine explorer Giovanni Verrazano described the native Americans in New York as handsome and tall in stature, "clothed with the feathers of birds of various colors," their hair "fastened back in a knot of olive color."

Fire Island Map Then & Now

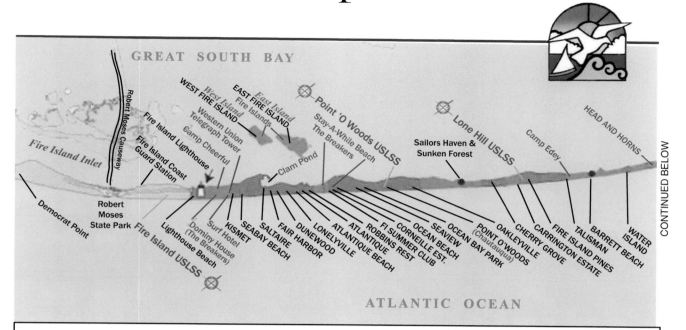

GREAT SOUTH BAY

Robert Moses Causeway

Fire Island Inlet

West Island WEST FIRE ISLAND
EAST FIRE ISLAND
East Island Fire Islands
Point 'O Woods USLSS
Stay-A-While Beach
The Breakers
Western Union Telegraph Tower
Camp Cheerful
Fire Island Lighthouse
Fire Island Coast Guard Station

Lone Hill USLSS
Sailors Haven & Sunken Forest
Camp Edey
HEAD AND HORNS

Democrat Point

Robert Moses State Park
Fire Island USLSS
Lighthouse Beach
Dominy House (The Breakers)
Surf Hotel
KISMET
SEABAY BEACH
SALTAIRE
FAIR HARBOR
DUNEWOOD
LONELYVILLE
ATLANTIQUE
ATLANTIQUE BEACH
ROBBINS REST
FI SUMMER CLUB
CORNEILLE EST.
OCEAN BEACH
SEAVIEW
OCEAN BAY PARK
POINT O'WOODS (Chautauqua)
OAKLEYVILLE
CHERRY GROVE
CARRINGTON ESTATE
FIRE ISLAND PINES
TALISMAN
BARRETT BEACH
WATER ISLAND

Clam Pond

CONTINUED BELOW

ATLANTIC OCEAN

The barrier beach has been known through the ages by many names. Long ago it was referred to as:
Prinse Maurits Eysland (Dutch 1600s), South Sand Beach, Great South Beach of Sand and Stones,
East Beach, South Beach, Raccoon Beach, Restless Isle, The Beach, Barrier Beach,
Fire Island and since 1964, Fire Island National Seashore.

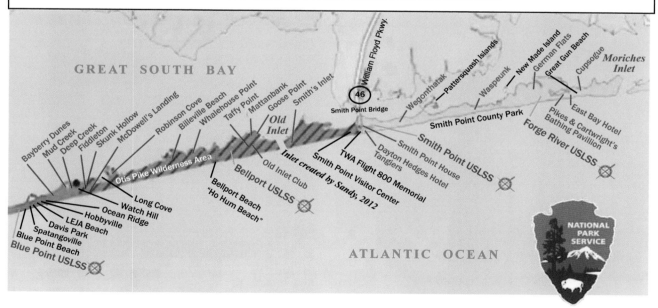

GREAT SOUTH BAY

William Floyd Pkwy.

New Made Island
German Flats
Great Gun Beach
Cupsogue
Moriches Inlet

Pattersquash Islands
Waspeunk
Wegonthatak

Bayberry Dunes
Mud Creek
Deep Creek
Fiddleton
Skunk Hollow
McDowell's Landing
Robinson Cove
Billeville Beach
Whalehouse Point
Taffy Point
Mattanbank
Goose Point
Smith's Inlet

46
Smith Point Bridge

Smith Point County Park

East Bay Hotel
Pikes & Cartwright's Bathing Pavillion

Forge River USLSS

Old Inlet

Otis Pike Wilderness Area
Old Inlet Club
Bellport USLSS
Bellport Beach "Ho Hum Beach"
Inlet created by Sandy, 2012
Smith Point Visitor Center
TWA Flight 800 Memorial
Dayton Hedges Hotel Tanglers
Smith Point House
Smith Point USLSS

Long Cove
Watch Hill
Ocean Ridge
Hobbyville
LEJA Beach
Davis Park
Spatangoville
Blue Point Beach
Blue Point USLSS

ATLANTIC OCEAN

NATIONAL PARK SERVICE

Communities are in approximate locations. Maps not to be used for navigational purposes.

Red type indicates communities which no longer exist.
Brown type indicates past United States Lifesaving Stations ⊗ and since 1915
    past Coast Guard stations which no longer exist.
Black indicates present day Fire Island
Green areas indicate Fire Island State, County and National Parks

Early Fashion Postcards

White Hotel, Water Island, 1919

Cupsogue Beach

Now known as Great Gun Beach, 1890

Early Cherry Grove, 1917

Boardwalk Point O' Woods, 1908

Sailing Party to Sammis Hotel, now Kismet, 1890

Midway Walk Ocean Beach, 1915

Saltaire Casino, 1914

Boating to Taffy Point, Fire Island, 1900s

Chapter V
Refrences and Appendix

New Surf Hotel Ocean Beach not to be confused with David Sammis's Surf Hotel early 1900s.
The New Surf Hotel was destroyed by a fire prior to 1920. In the foreground is the
Chesapeake wooden ferry in the Ocean Beach basin early 1900s.

"A reader lives a thousand lives before he dies . . .The man who never reads lives only one."
– George R.R. Martin

History Books & Appendix of LI

"In a certain sense all men are historians"
Caryle *Essays on History*

The author has not burdened the reader with constant mention of authorities, or with an acknowledgement of his great debt to early writers, mapmakers or cartographers. The books and manuscripts chiefly consulted are named in this appendix. As far as possible facts have been taken from original sources and those that are not accurate historically had not been used as a foundation. All others have been judiciously corroborated.

Forge River Lifesaving Station #19, across from Mastic Beach. Built in 1871, closed in 1947.

Forge River, launching the lifeboat.

1648 – The Colony of New Netherland, A Dutch Settlement in Seventeenth Century America - by Jaap, Jacobs

1670 – A Brief Description of New York Formerly Called New Amsterdam – Daniel Denton

1786 – The American Young Man's Best Companion Containing Spelling - by George Fisher

1815 – American Coast Pilot – by Edmund M. Blunt

1825 – American Coast Pilot - by Edmund M. Blunt (Principal Harbors and Capes)

1828 – Sketch of The First Settlement of Long Island – Silas Wood (first history of L.I.)

1833 – Principal Harbors and Capes – Edmund M. Blunt

1834 – Army and Navy Chronicle 1834 – by F.R. Hassler (Fire Island Beach)

1835 – Fire Island Anals -The American Monthly Magazine – by D.K. Minor and T.C. Wood

1839 – Vol. I - 1843 – Vol. II Long Island from Its Discovery and Settlement to the Present Time -
        by Benjamin F. Thompson Counsellor at Law

1845 – History of New Netherland or New York Under the Dutch – by E.B. O'Callaghan 1492 - 1646

1845 – History of Long Island – Nathaniel S. Prime - From its first settlement by Europeans, to the year 1845

1849 – Revolutionary Incidents of Suffolk & Kings Counties – by Henry Onderdonk Jr. (1st to mention FI Inlet 1778)

1851 – Pictorial Field Book of the Revolution - by Benson J. Lossing

1853 – History of the State of New York – by John Broadhead

1859 – Gazetteer of the State of New York – by John Homer French

1861 – Memoir Northern Atlantic Ocean - by Alexander G. Findlay (London)

1864 – Calendar of N.Y. Colonial Manuscripts in the Office of the Secretary of State 1643 – 1803

1865 – Early History of Suffolk County L.I. - by Hon. Henry Nicoll

1868 – Historical Manuscripts Relating to the War of the Revolution – Secretary of State Vol. 1

1879 – History of New York During the Revolutionary War - by Thomas Jones

1874 – Sketches of Suffolk County – Richard M Bayles (Historical Outline of Long Island)

1875 – Antiquities of Long Island - by Gabriel Furman

1880 – Records of the Town of Brookhaven Book A. 1657 – 1679 and 1790 – 1798

1882 – History of Suffolk County and New York – W.W. Munsell and Co.

1885 – Bi-Centennial – History of Suffolk County – Budget Steam Print

1886 – Love and Luck – by Robert Barnwell Roosevelt

1889 – Huntington Town Records including Babylon 1776 to 1873 – Introduction by Charles R. Strteet

1896 – Early Long Island – A Colonial Study by Martha Bockee Flint

1897 – Early Long Island Wills of Suffolk County 1691 – 1703 by Francis P. Harper 1897

1898 – Silas Wood's Sketch of Town of Huntington L.I. -
      Edited with Geneological & Historical Notes by William Smith Pelletreau, a.m.

1899 – Vol. 1 & Vol. 2 - The Dutch and Quaker Colonies in America - by John Fiske

1902 – Vol. 1 & Vol. 2 - A History of Long Island - by Peter Ross

1902 – Historic Long Island – by Rufus Rockwell Wilson

1902 – A Documentary History – Queens – Nassau – Long Island - by Henry A. Stoutenburg

1911 – Indian Place – Names – On Long Island and Islands Adjacent – William Wallace Tooker

1914 – Geology of Long Island New York – by Myron L. Fuller

1915 – Babylon and Fire Island – by A. Wittemann – Published by Long Island News Co.

1918 – History of Southampton – by James Truslow Adams

1921 – Evolution of Long Island – Ralph Henry Gabriel

1949 – Long Island a History of Nassau and Suffolk – Paul Bailey

1966 – Long Island Discovery – Seon Manley

1975 – A History of the Sayville Community (including Fire Island) Charles P. Dickerson

1976 – First History of West Islip – by Gerald and Judith Wilcox

1982 – Storms, Ships & Surfman – The Life-Savers of Fire Island – Ellice B. Gonzalez

1983 – Fire Island 1650s – 1980s - by Madeleine C. Johnson

1983 – Suffolk County Tercentenary Commission (Town of Islip Section)

1983 – Fire Island Recollection – Histories of the Island Fire Island Association

1986 – Huntington Book of Transcription 1657 – 1745

Fire Island State Park, NY with the flag, 1905 Lighthouse in the background.

1988 – Long Island Studies – Evoking a Sense of Place – Joann P. Krieg

1997 – Long Island Maps and Their Makers: Five Centuries of Cartographic History - by David Yehling Allen

2008 – A Description of New Netherland – (Reprint) Adriaen Van Der Donck (Author) Charles T. Gehring

2010 – The Bay Men – A Clammer's Story – by Evert Bay Scott

2011 – Reminiscing About Ocean Beach and Fire Island – by Cheryl Dunbar Kahlke

2013 – A Short Bright Flash – by Theresa Levitt

2016 – In Praise of Poison Ivy – Anita Sanchez

2017 – Department of the Interior, U.S. Geological Survey – "Wilderness Breach"

Long Island Forum

The Magazine of Long Island's History & Heritage

The Western Union Telegraph tower was built in 1876 east of the Surf Hotel. It was five stories high and later an eight story lookout was added. It closed in 1920 and was destroyed in the hurricane of 1938.

"Mistakes remembered are not faults forgot" R.H. Newell *Colimbia's Agony*

Map Directory

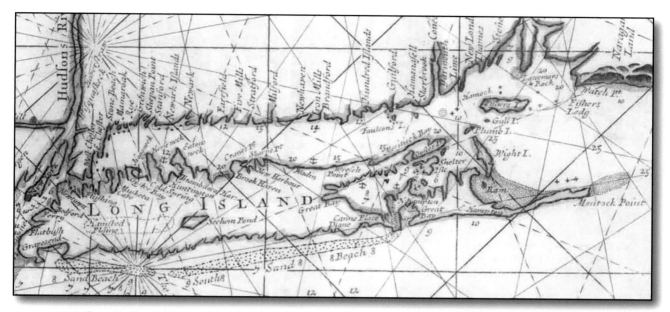

1706 South Sand Beach – Author Unknown – Showing Fire Island as a Penninsula

Time Line of Fire Island Inlet

Left is the Sammis Hotel, 1889 - present day west of Kismet. Drifting through the inlet at sunset is a sailing ship.

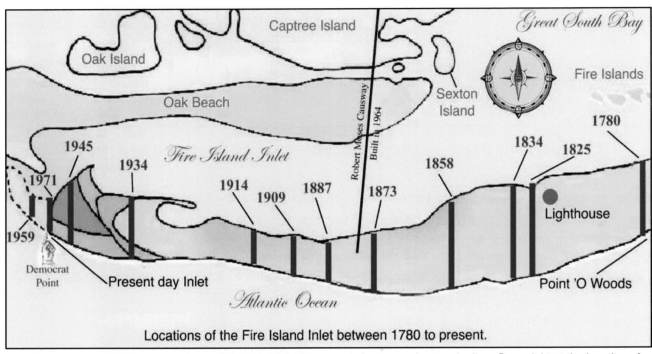

Locations of the Fire Island Inlet between 1780 to present.

Over the last 250 years, the landfill on Fire Island Inlet has traveled westward several miles. Once right at the location of Chautauqua (Point 'O Woods) it has now moved westerly to Democrat Point. The south "Thumb" of sand (shown on the left in yellow) was removed by Federal dredging in 1959 and deposited on the Oak Beach shore, only to return periodically.

The movement of the Fire Island Inlet has been under scrutiny since it first broke through in the storm of 1690 to 1691. The early British war maps show an inlet referred to as the Blue Point Inlet and the Fire Island Inlet utilized for navigation. Following the sequence, we know that the inlet in 1825 was in the physical position next to the lighthouse.

The first study of the inlet under the Rivers and Harbors Act of 1905 had been authorized to construct a breakwater. The engineers reporting to the War Department in 1906 agreed that it was not advisable for the United States to undertake a breakwater construction.

There is no question about the migration of Fire Island westward, a distance of 4.6 miles between 1825 and 1940 when the movement was finally halted by the construction of the jetty at Point Democrat.

In the early summer of 1941 a stone jetty 4,800 feet long was completed at Democrat Point at the extreme westerly end of the barrier beach. This jetty was constructed by the federal government in cooperation with the Long Island State Park Commission and the County of Suffolk to stop the westward accretion of Fire Island and to stabilize the inlet.

The question of permanent stabilization and maintenance of the navigation channel through Fire Island Inlet is still to be solved. Dredging is to serve only as a stopgap. There is only one logical way to cope with this problem and that is under the orderly process of federal procedures of the Corps of Engineers and Rivers and Harbors Act of Congress.